Raising Milk Goats Successfully

Gail Luttmann

WILLIAMSON PUBLISHING
CHARLOTTE, VERMONT 05445

Library of Congress Cataloging-in-Publication Data

Luttmann, Gail.
  Raising milk goats successfully.

  Bibliography: p.
  Includes index.
  1. Goats. I. Title.
SF383.L88 1986 636.3'9142 86-26694
ISBN 0-913589-24-1

Cover and interior design: Trezzo-Braren Studio
Typography: Villanti & Sons Printers, Inc.
Printing: Capital City Press

Williamson Publishing Co.
Charlotte, Vermont 05445

Manufactured in the United States of America

10 9 8 7 6 5

Dedication

Dedicated to a certain capricious creature whose whim it was to materialize in an open kitchen window, delighting a four-year-old at lunch and initiating the lifelong love of caprines that led to this book.

(Photo by Matto)

Acknowledgements _____ 6

Chapter 1 _____ 7
GETTING STARTED

Chapter 2 _____ 21
HOUSING

Chapter 3 _____ 31
DAIRY GOAT RATIONS

Chapter 4 _____ 43
NUTRITIONAL NEEDS

Chapter 5 _____ 53
DAIRY GOAT MANAGEMENT

Chapter 6 _____ 65
CHOOSING DAMS AND SIRES

Chapter 7 _____ 75
BREEDING AND KIDDING

Chapter 8 _____ 87
KID CARE

Contents

Chapter 9 _____ 101
GOAT MILK

Chapter 10 _____ 113
UDDER CARE

Chapter 11 _____ 121
HEALTH CARE

Chapter 12 _____ 127
TROUBLE SHOOTING

Chapter 13 _____ 137
ADDITIONAL GOATKEEPING BENEFITS

Chapter 14 _____ 147
RUNNING YOUR DAIRY BUSINESS

Appendixes _____ 157
   A. BOOKS, SUPPLIES, SERVICES
   B. GOATKEEPERS' JARGON

Index _____ 169

Acknowledgements

Thanks to the many who helped with this book, and special thanks to—

The cheesemakers at Le Chevrier in Monroe, Tennessee, for allowing many interruptions to their busy goat-milk cheese and yogurt making schedule;

Betty Winters and the Cub Hollow Dairy Goats of Gainesboro, Tennessee, for patience;

Temple Grandin, livestock handling specialist, University of Illinois, for sharing stress-reducing techniques;

Jenny Sisco, Black Shire Registered Pygmy Goats, Coldwater, Michigan; Alice Hall, author of *The Pygmy Goat in America*; and the Robert Johnson family of Pine Cone Valley Goat Farm, Rossville, Georgia, for details on raising Pygmies;

George F. W. Haenlein, dairy goat specialist, University of Delaware, for information on nutrition and other aspects of dairy goat management;

John C. Porter, Extension dairy specialist, Penacook, New Hampshire, for clear and comprehensive details on dairy procedures;

Forest Felling, Country Computing consultation service, Bridgeton, Indiana, for information on software for dairy goats;

And Matto, the photographer, for patiently taking "just one more shot of that goat over there."

Chapter 1

GETTING STARTED

The usefulness of goats as dairy animals was recognized long before recorded history. Goats, together with dogs, were the first animals to be domesticated. They are mentioned several times in the Bible, and were carried on sailing ships as a sure source of fresh milk by early explorers, including Columbus and Captain Cook.

Today, more than half the world's population drinks goat milk. Most Americans have not tasted this nutritious beverage, but that seems about to change. According to the latest USDA livestock census, the goat population rose nearly 200 percent since the census four years previous. And the popularity of dairy goats is still growing, due to our ever-increasing awareness of health and nutrition, and to our desire to enjoy more foods that are traditional in other countries.

If you plan to join the growing numbers of dairy goat herders, this book will tell you how to choose a milk goat, feed her for optimum production, and keep her healthy and contented. You'll learn to breed her for a regular milk flow, care for her newborn kids, and turn surplus stock into meat for your family or cash to cover herd upkeep.

When you finish this book, you'll know proper milking techniques, how to handle milk to keep it sweet tasting, and how to make such wholesome dairy products as yogurt and cheese. You'll be convinced, as I am, that dairy goats are affectionate, gentle, quick learners, and fun to be around.

So let's get started!

WHAT BREED?

There are six officially recognized breeds of dairy goat—Alpine, LaMancha, Nubian, Oberhasli, Toggenburg, and Saanen—and a miniature one, the Pygmy. Of the six larger breeds, four are closely related and look quite similar. Alpines, Oberhasli, Saanens, and Toggenburgs all originated in the Alps of France and Switzerland. As a group they are referred to as the Swiss breeds. All have straight or slightly concave faces—called dished—upright ears, and an alert, deerlike appearance.

Nubians and LaManchas were developed by crossing Swiss goats with other types. The Nubian has ancestry in Egyptian and Indian breeds, while the LaMancha was bred from Spanish goats. The Nubian averages less milk than other large breeds. LaManchas, Saanens, and Oberhasli are high yield milkers.

Pygmies, Nubians, and LaManchas are considered the desert breeds. Pygmies give an amazing quantity of high quality milk, and put on flesh very rapidly for their small size. The growth characteristics of all three of the desert breeds make them suitable as meat animals as well as milkers. Milk from Pygmies and Nubians averages highest in butterfat and is therefore best for cheese, butter, and ice cream.

Nubians and LaManchas do best in warmer areas. Nubians, in fact, are subject to frostbitten ears when temperatures really dip. Pygmies originated in hot, humid climates and prefer that kind of weather. But because their housing needs are so easily met, they are also a good choice for extremely cold areas where goats must be housed indoors much of the year. All of the Swiss breeds do well in cold climates, but the Toggenburg perhaps adapts most easily to very cold weather without slowing down in milk production.

Alpine

You can recognize an Alpine by its large, angular appearance and long, slender neck. Alpines are a variety of colors and combinations designated by French and Swiss terms such as *cou blanc* and *sundgau*. In most, the front quarters are one color and the hindquarters another.

LaMancha

The LaMancha is the only totally American goat, having its origins on the West Coast. LaManchas can be nearly any color, and are distinguished from other breeds by the absence, or near absence, of external ears. If there is little or no cartilage, the ear is called "gopher." Bucks used for breeding should have gopher ears, and to be registered they must. A small ear with a bit of cartilage is called "elf." Female LaManchas may have either elf or gopher ears. This is perhaps the most docile breed.

Nubian

The Nubian is by far the most popular breed in the United States today. This goat can be recognized by the rounded shape of its face — called a Roman nose — and its floppy ears. Nubians may be many colors and patterns, but are usually black, tan, or bay (red), sometimes with spots like a painted horse. Nubians are more restless than other breeds, and tend to be more vociferous.

Oberhasli

Until 1978, when Oberhasli were officially recognized as a separate breed, they were called Swiss Alpines. They come in shades of bay with black markings. Though they are one of the oldest established breeds in Switzerland, there are few of them in this country.

Pygmy

Pygmies are ideal for those with limited space or limited milk needs. On the average, Pygmies give about one-third as much as larger does. Although their milk is rather high in butterfat content, much of the cream separates out within a day and can be skimmed off easily. Pygmies can be many colors, but shades of grey, especially salt-and-pepper, called *agouti*, are most common. Pygmies are blocky, deep, and wide in contrast to the lean, angular look of other dairy breeds. In California, they are popular as housepets.

Angular Alpines are often two colors, one in the front, the other in the rear. (Photo by Matto)

LaManchas have very short ears or none at all. (Photo by Matto)

Nubians can be identified by their long, floppy ears. (Photo by Matto)

The Oberhasli has a bay coat set off with black markings. (Photo by Matto)

As this yearling doe shows, Pygmies are proportionately blockier and have shorter legs than their larger cousins. (Photo courtesy of Dewey Meadows Farm, Rome, New York)

The all-white Saanen holds the world record for milk production. (Photo by Matto)

Saanen

As of this writing, an Australian Saanen holds the world record for goat milk production, with 7714 pounds in 365 days to her credit. Saanens are all-white, or sometimes a light cream. A Saanen of any other color—usually black, and sometimes with white markings—is called a Sable.

Toggenburg

Toggenburgs are the smallest of the Swiss breeds. They are solid shades of brown, ranging from fawn to dark chocolate, with crisp white markings on the face and legs. Toggenburg milk averages lowest in butterfat.

You can recognize a Toggenburg by its brown coat with snappy white trim. (Photo by Matto)

BREED COMPARISON

Breed	Characteristics	Size and Weight		Average Production	
Alpine	Erect ears; long, slender neck; all colors, usually two-tone	Doe: Buck:	30", 135# min. 32", 170# min.	milk: butterfat:	1500–1600# 3.5%
LaMancha	Very short or no ears; all colors; very docile	Doe: Buck:	28", 130# min. 30", 160# min.	milk: butterfat:	1800# 4%
Nubian	Roman nose and long, droopy ears; black, tan, shades of bay; somewhat restless	Doe: Buck:	30", 135# min. 32", 170# min.	milk: butterfat:	1300–1500# 4.5–5%
Oberhasli	Erect ears; shades of bay trimmed in black	Doe: Buck:	28", 120# min. 30", 150# min.	milk: butterfat:	2000# 3.5–4%
Pygmy	Erect ears; miniature size; usually grey, sometimes caramel, rarely chocolate	Doe: Buck:	16–22.4", 55# 16–23.6", 80#	milk: butterfat:	610–760# 4–6.5%
Saanen	Erect ears; all white or cream	Doe: Buck:	30", 135# min. 32", 170# min.	milk: butterfat:	1800–2000# 3.5%
Toggenburg	Erect ears; shades of brown trimmed with white	Doe: Buck:	26", 120# min. 28", 150# min.	milk: butterfat:	1500–1600# 3.3–3.5%

CHOOSING A DAIRY GOAT

Pick a breed whose appearance appeals to you. You'll be looking at your herd at least twice a day when you milk and feed, so you may as well enjoy the view. Whether you get registered purebreds depends on your purpose in having goats. If you plan to show them, or hope to get top dollar for your surplus kids, you should have registration papers.

Grade goats look like purebreds, but have only one parent that's pure while the other is of mixed or unknown ancestry. Grade goats are usually cheaper than purebreds, but may give more milk if bred for production rather than appearance.

Mixed breed goats will rarely have predictable milking and breeding characteristics, and scrub goats—those of completely unknown ancestry—are not good dairy animals. Start with the best goats you can afford to avoid future disappointment in milking and breeding results.

Healthy goats will show curiosity over your visit. (Photo by Matto)

Checking the Goat

Before you purchase a goat, check it over carefully. It should not have horns, which can injure you and other goats. It should stand squarely and walk freely without lameness. Improper hoof trimming, foot infection, or deformed feet can cause limping. Watch for upper and lower jaws that don't meet, indicating possible eating problems. Run your hands over the goat's body to check for lumps, knots, sores, scabs, and scars.

Examine the teeth as a sign of age. A goat has eight teeth at the front of its lower jaw. If the middle two are large, the animal is one year old. If it has four large teeth, it's two years old; if six, it is three or four; and if all eight are large, the animal is four or five. Eight large teeth that are excessively worn or separating means the goat is quite old. A prime dairy goat is not more than four years old.

Look over the mother, father, siblings, and aunts, if possible, for good health and uniformity in the family line. Peek into the housing for cleanliness, indicating a caring owner and the likelihood that the animals are healthy. If the goat you choose has bright eyes and shows curiosity over your visit, it is probably a healthy one.

GOOD DAIRY CHARACTER

Part	Description
Jaw	Strong, neither overshot nor undershot
Neck	Long, lean, smoothly blending into shoulders
Back	Straight, slight break at hip to slope toward tail
Ribs	Wide apart, well-rounded with large barrel
Pelvis	Large
Legs	Strong, sturdy, straight, wide apart
Udder	Soft, wide, evenly hung, held high
Skin	Pliable with fine textured hair

DAIRY CHARACTER

A doe's appearance is a good indication of her milking abilities, or dairy character. A good milker should be lean and angular. You may think she looks undernourished if you're inexperienced with dairy goats, but a thick or stocky doe may have trouble breeding and kidding, and will not milk well. Unless she's a Pygmy! Then she should have the stocky look typical of Pygmies.

Examining the Udder

One of the most important features of a doe is her udder. If you're looking at a doeling, lift her hind legs and examine the little teats. There should be two, and only two, and they should be wide apart. If the doe is older and has a mature udder, ask to have her put on a milking stand so you can make a thorough examination. Her udder should be large and round, with smooth, elastic skin and no sores, scars, or lumps. It should be high and wide and not hang lower than the rear hocks. Otherwise the doe may get her legs tangled up in it, or bang it when she walks.

There should be two well-defined teats, one on each side. Each should have a single opening that passes a good stream of milk. You should be able to grasp the teat in your whole hand for all breeds but the Pygmy, in which the teats should be large enough to milk with two fingers and a thumb.

If possible, milk the doe or watch her being milked. Try to go for two consecutive milkings so you can see if the doe was *bagged up,* which means her previous milking was skipped to make you think she gives more than she really does. Taste the milk to make sure you like it. Milk flavor is influenced by the doe's rations and her condition of health, but also varies between the breeds and even among individual does. If you don't like the way it tastes, keep shopping.

Check Milking Records

If everything looks good so far, ask to see the doe's milking records, which should be entered in pounds and tenths of a pound for accuracy. At her prime, a large doe should give at least eight pounds, or around a gallon a day from about two weeks after the beginning of lactation, and for the next fifteen weeks. Then she'll gradually taper off to about two pounds or one quart a day. Younger and older does should give at least six pounds a day at their peak. A Pygmy will average about one-third the amount given by a larger doe. Some goats do better than average for their breed, but you'll pay a lot more for them. Don't waste time and money on a doe that gives much less.

HOW MANY, WHAT AGE?

Goats are social animals with strong herd instincts. They get lonely and into trouble when kept alone. It takes at least two to keep each other company. If one doe is enough to satisfy your household milk needs, consider keeping her kids with her until she gives birth again the following year, or get a disbudded wether—a castrated buck—to keep her company.

The big question for beginners is what age to get. If you start with kids, get them at least three weeks old so you'll know they're growing strong and healthy. Since young animals are hard to check for dairy character, look over the mother and older siblings by the same sire. Taste the mother's milk to make sure you like it.

Starting with kids gives you the fun of watching them grow up. But it also means that you'll have to wait more than a year for your first drop of milk. Starting with bred does gives you several weeks to get to know your goats before they have to be milked. As soon as they give birth, you'll have the double pleasure of newborn kids and fresh milk.

Get a written guarantee that the doe is pregnant. There are mail-in pregnancy tests that let you find out for sure. If the doe turns out not to be with kid, or aborts, the guarantee will allow you to get her rebred at no charge. Also get a Service Memorandum. This is documentation of the kid's sire and the mating date.

By starting with a milker, you can check the doe's milking and kidding records. She'll be trained to the milk stand, making it easier for you if you're inexperienced. If you need milking instructions, ask the seller to give you a lesson so you won't damage your new doe's udder.

Since you should have at least two goats, you can mix and match them by starting with a milker and her most recent kid, or a milker and a bred doe. If you get goats of different ages, or from different herds, they'll fight to establish which will be the boss. Prevent serious injury by keeping them in individual stalls where they can communicate through a separating partition.

BUCK SELECTION

A buck requires all the same care, grooming, hoof trimming, pen cleaning, and feeding as a doe, but produces no milk. He must be kept in separate housing, away from the milkers, so he won't impart an off-flavor to their milk. Many herders don't keep a buck. Breeding services are readily available in most areas through sire services and artificial insemination. They are often cheaper than owning all the appropriate bucks, since the same buck may not be suitable for every doe in your herd. Furthermore, as the successive generations of does improve in milk production, they should be mated to better and better bucks.

Some herders find that owning one of those delightfully uninhibited creatures is half the fun of having goats. The keeper of a fairly large herd may feel that having a good buck or two saves time and money in mating services. If you choose to own a buck, wait until you've had your does awhile so you'll know what to look for in a mate for them.

If you start with a buckling, you can raise him to be gentle. On the other hand, getting a proven buck assures that he's got what it takes. Look for a buck with the characteristics of a good dairy animal. In addition, he should have firm, oblong testicles. The ladies in his immediate family should be better milkers than the does in your herd.

Your buck will need a companion. If you keep two bucks, they'll get along better if they were raised together. A buck's buddy can also be a wether, or a non-producing doe. A buck kept by himself soon gets into all sorts of mischief.

WHERE TO BUY

Herd disposal sales are a constant fact of life in the dairy goat world. Life styles change so that the milking of goats may no longer fit in. Sometimes a herder will decide to specialize in a different breed. Whatever the reason for a herd sale, it's one of the best ways to buy good dairy goats for a good price.

If you don't intend to show, or you're willing to wait and breed your own show quality animals, another way to strike a bargain is to purchase a less than perfect one. For example, a doe may have a non-heritable injury that affects her appearance and price, but not her producing abilities. Sometimes a particular mating produces kids that are perfectly fine, but of a color that doesn't appeal to the owner. To find such bargains, and to determine the current going rate for dairy goats, shop around and talk to the various goatkeepers in your area.

Among the best ways to find goats for sale is through a local goat club or goat show. Both give you the chance to meet goatkeepers who care about their animals. These people like to talk about goats, answer questions, and especially see that beginners get off to a good start. When you attend shows with stiff competition, you'll learn quickly who has the best goats.

You can locate nearby goatkeepers through the membership lists of the various national registries or from the national club promoting the breed you're most interested in. Addresses for these organizations are given at the back of this book.

The worst place to buy a goat is at a livestock auction. These goats are under a lot of stress, may pick up diseases from each other, and were probably brought to the auction because the owner didn't think much of them.

Private sales cause the least stress to dairy goats, letting them adjust more quickly to their new home. You can ask the seller for some of the goat's usual rations, so you can switch to the new diet gradually. You'll also be able to have the animal's hooves trimmed, hornbuds of kids removed, and young males castrated, if necessary, so you won't have to perform these operations while your animals are still getting used to you, and you to them.

HOME AT LAST

Being well prepared ensures that your initial goat owning experience will go smoothly. Have housing, feeders, waterers, and fencing in place before you bring home the first animal. If you buy milkers, set up a milk stand as well. Be sure to stock up on plenty of feed.

Being moved to a new home is a stressful experience for dairy goats. Help reduce stress by spending time with them. They enjoy being brushed, and if you talk gently while you work it will help calm them, as well as teach them to recognize your voice.

During the initial get-acquainted period, your goats may be quite vocal, expecially if they are mothers taken away from their kids. But as they get used to their new surroundings and your routine, most will settle down to become an enjoyable part of your everyday life.

Chapter 2

HOUSING

Goats do not require elaborate and expensive housing. Their needs are easily met by a simple shelter that is dry, well-ventilated, draft-free, and easy to clean. Goats are most comfortable at temperatures between 55°F and 70°F. They do fine down to 0°F, but at 80°F and above they begin to suffer. In southern and western areas, housing is needed to keep goats cool during summer, while in the North, a shelter must keep them warm in winters.

The simplest and healthiest shelter is a three-sided one, facing south. Sliding doors on the open wall can be installed to shut out bad weather. In areas where extreme cold is likely, a barn may be necessary. Such a structure requires tight construction to avoid drafts, and good ventilation to prevent moisture build-up. Windows aid air circulation and let in warm, cheerful sunlight. The herd will produce its own heat; auxiliary heat is both unnecessary and unhealthy. Provide doors that swing freely to an adjoining yard so the animals can wander in and out.

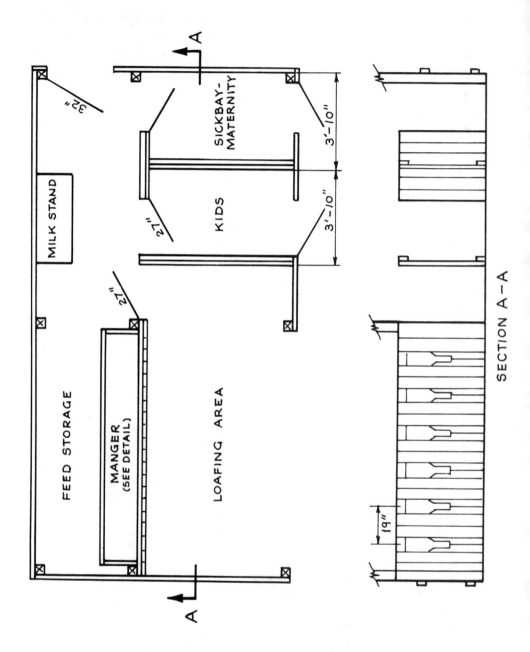

FEED STORAGE

MILK STAND

MANGER
(SEE DETAIL)

27"

32"

LOAFING AREA

A

A

SICKBAY-
MATERNITY

KIDS

27"

3'-10"

3'-10"

SECTION A-A

19"

Open housing plan for a small herd.

For both types of shelter, floors may be packed dirt, sand, or concrete. Slatted wooden platforms may be added to keep the goats off damp, dirty bedding. Platforms should be constructed with removable sections for easy cleaning. Design the roof to keep climbers off, and add eave gutters to channel away rain water.

The shelter can have an open central area or a series of stalls. Some goatkeepers prefer individual stalls for control over feeding and to encourage better milk production by preventing quarrels. In any case, you will need some stalls for kidding does, newborn kids, injured animals, and timid ones which have trouble competing with bullies.

MANGERS

A trough that holds feed for livestock is called a *manger*. Properly designed mangers are durable, easy to clean, and minimize feed wastage and contamination. Goats like to pick through hay looking for the choicest morsels. When they get a mouthful, they pull back and scatter much of it on the floor, where it gets trampled. In addition, they tend to put their front hooves up on anything that gives them a foothold, damaging flimsy equipment as well as dropping manure and bits of dirty bedding into the feed. Low feeders also become victims to the occasional load of goat berries.

The classic goat feeder is the keyhole manger with access along an outside aisle. (Photo by Matto)

Keyhole mangers are the classic goat feeders. A keyhole opening provides a slot through which the goat must put his head to reach the feed. A series of keyholes allows goats to eat individually without interference from others. Placed against an outside wall, or along the aisle adjoining a series of stalls, a row of mangers simplifies feeding. In addition to one keyhole per goat for all-day access to hay, you need extra ones for salt, baking soda, and water. Bucks also need a trough for grain. Does usually eat theirs on the milk stand.

Provide separate mangers for kids where they can enjoy their hay and other rations away from older ones, preferably in a private stall.

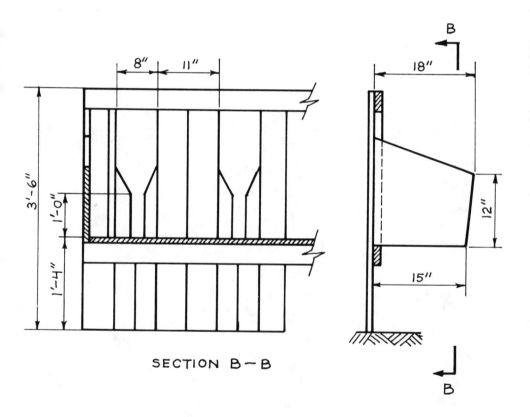

SECTION B—B

Manger construction.

WATERERS

For good milk production, goats need access to pure water at all times. The only truly sensible way to water them is with an automatic watering device. On-demand nipple waterers are available from dairy goat supply houses, and so are bowls that fill automatically as they are drawn down. Both require a pressurized water line to the goat shelter.

If you don't have running water, you'll have to carry water at least twice a day. Water your herd in a fairly deep container with access through a keyhole to eliminate contamination and spillage. Do not use a bucket with a handle that might get caught over a goat's head.

Supply good drainage around waterers since some goats tend to drip when they drink. Where water freezes in winter, electricity in the housing will allow you to use a water warming device.

FEED STORAGE

In addition to stalls, mangers, and waterers, your goat shelter should have space for feed storage. Just how much room you need depends on both the size of your herd and how often you bring in supplies.

Hay may be stored in an extra stall, in a loft, or in an adjoining lean-to. It should never be placed on the ground, where soil moisture will spoil the bottom layers. You can save as much as 15 percent in lost hay by putting down pallets, old tires, wooden poles, plastic sheets, or crushed rock before you stack the bales. Never store hay outdoors in the weather, where it will lose much of its nutritive value.

Grain is best kept in galvanized or tough plastic garbage containers with tight-fitting lids to keep it clean and safe from rodents. Either chain and lock down the lids or keep the containers where they'll be secure from the herd. The moment your goats learn where you keep the grain, they'll do everything in their power to sneak in and gorge themselves. Containers are usually safe in a closed stall with the hay, in a separate area adjoining the shelter, or in the milk parlor where they'll be handy at milking time.

MILK PARLOR

The milking room, commonly called a *parlor*, is most convenient when it adjoins the dairy shelter. For the sake of clean, tasty milk, it should be isolated to keep out dust and wandering animals. The parlor should be easy to clean, something that's facilitated by a concrete floor with a central drain. Windows create a cheerful, sunlit atmosphere, and screens keep out summer flies. Running water should be handy for rinsing equipment and washing hands.

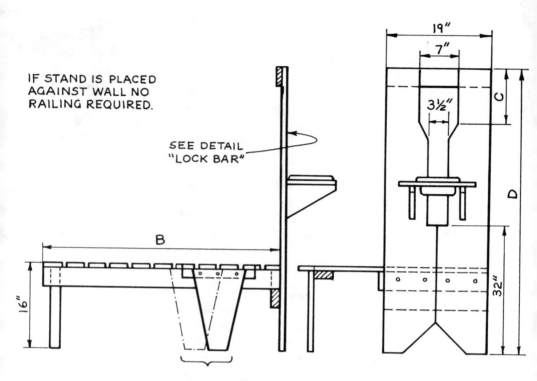

IF STAND IS PLACED
AGAINST WALL NO
RAILING REQUIRED.

SEE DETAIL
"LOCK BAR"

19"

7"

3½"

C

D

32"

B

16"

SEAT SHOWN IN POSITION
FOR PERSON 5'-4" OR TALLER.
FOR PERSON, SHORTER MOVE SEAT
ONE BOARD AWAY FROM STANCHION.

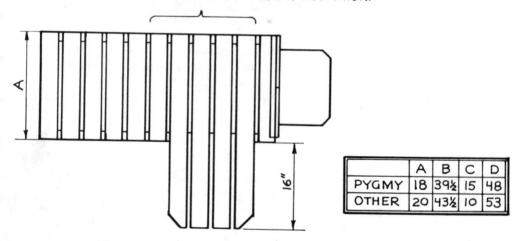

A

16"

	A	B	C	D
PYGMY	18	39½	15	48
OTHER	20	43½	10	53

Milk stand construction.

The milking parlor should be at least five feet by eight feet to allow enough space for the milk stand, a supply cabinet, a sink, and a scale to weigh the milk. You may want to make it a little larger if you store grain containers there.

If you're considering going commercial, check with your state Extension dairy specialist and the dairy inspector from your state's Division of Food and Dairies for legal requirements before you construct new facilities or remodel existing buildings.

MILK STAND

A milk stand is a platform on which a doe is restrained at a height that makes it comfortable for you to milk her. It can be used at other times, such as when you trim hooves or give shots. A keyhole stanchion holds the goat's head, and a dish of grain keeps her busy while you work.

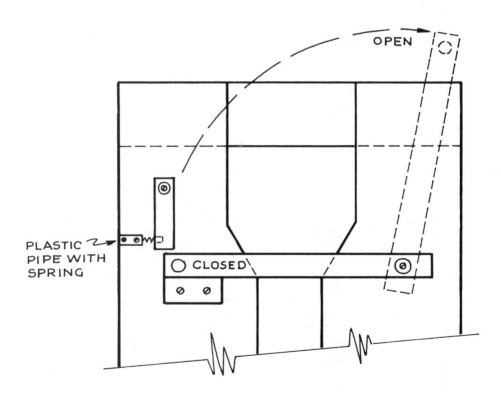

OPEN

PLASTIC
PIPE WITH
SPRING

CLOSED

Detail of lockbar at head of milk stand.

The height of the stand depends on your size and personal com-
fort—fifteen to eighteen inches is standard. Some stands have a sloped
runway, which is unnecessary unless the stand is unusually high or your
does have very low hanging udders that easily get injured. If you use
a runway, cross it with non-skid cleats.

Place the milk stand where the does can jump up directly on enter-
ing the parlor. If you have only a few goats, you can have them enter
and leave through the same door. If you have lots of ladies milling
around while they wait their turn, it's easier to have them enter one
door and exit by another into a separate area.

YARD

Goats are active and enjoy the freedom to wander around. Unless
they're fenced in, they'll make short work of your garden, young fruit
trees, and ornamental shrubbery. A fenced yard should adjoin the shelter so the goats can meander in and out. Some keepers walk their herds
to a distant pasture to forage during the day, in which case only a small
yard is needed for days when conditions are not suitable for foraging.

Have the yard on the south side of the shelter where the sun can
sanitize it and keep it dry. A gentle slope provides better drainage and
helps prevent foot rot and other unhealthy conditions. If the land is
level or drainage is poor, consider paving at least a portion of the yard
so the animals will have a dry place to stand. Paving also keeps hooves
worn down so they'll need less frequent trimming. A low concrete
ledge or a boulder in the yard helps wear down hooves, and provides
the opportunity for exercise. If you're handy with wood, you might construct an exercise platform for your goats to play on.

FENCES AND GATES

Goats are about the most difficult of all livestock to keep penned in.
Their curiosity, coupled with their agility, will test your ingenuity in
keeping them where they'll be safe from predators and your valuable
vegetation will be safe from them. Goats love to stand on their hind legs
with their front hooves resting on fence-tops while they peer out, crush-
ing down loose fencing until eventually they can step over it.

Traditional goat fencing is made from woven wire four to five feet
high, against seven-foot posts on twelve-foot centers. A strand of electrified wire twelve inches from the top, and another twelve inches from
the bottom on the inside, prevent climbing and leaning. Barbed wire
should not be used because goats too easily get tangled in it and suffer
torn ears, udders, and other parts.

The most effective and economical fencing is New Zealand style, or smooth-wire high-tensile electric fencing. It costs about half the price of any other type of fence, can be used on level or rough terrain, is easy to maintain, and may be combined with existing fences. The greater tensile strength of the strands allows you to pull them tighter than other types of wire, eliminating sagging. The energizing unit effectively charges miles of wire and does not ground out as easily as other fence chargers when touched by invading weeds. Sources of supplies are given at the back of this book.

Getting through fences isn't all goats are good at. They're also notorious gate-crashers. Some of the tricks used by goatkeepers to foil freedom-seeking goats are having the gates open inward, using heavy springs that automatically snap gates shut, putting latches half-way down on the outside of the gate where goats have trouble reaching them, and cross-tying gates on the outside so goats can't climb up on the bracing. Never top gates or fences with pickets since heads and hooves too easily get stuck in them.

HOUSING REQUIREMENTS

Type	Per Large Goat	Per Pygmy
DOES		
Open housing	15 sq. ft.	10 sq. ft.
Stalls	6×6 ft.	5×5 ft.
Stall partition height	3.5 ft.	3 ft.
Milk parlor	5×8 ft. min.	same
Yard	200 sq. ft.	130 sq. ft.
Minimum exercise area*	50 sq. ft.	40 sq. ft.
Fence height	5 ft.	4 ft.
BUCKS		
Housing	40 sq. ft.	30 sq. ft.
Stall partition height	5 ft.	4 ft.
Yard	100 sq. ft.	70 sq. ft.
Fence height	6 ft.	5 ft.

*Minimum exercise area applies when goats may be confined indoors for long periods due to bad weather, or are occasionally kept in small yards when normally they would be out foraging.

House bucks at least fifty feet from the milking does, and preferably downwind, to keep their seasonal odor from getting into the milk, and to prevent them from becoming overly excited during breeding season. Bucks need the same clean, dry housing as does, with plenty of fresh air and sunshine.

Provide individual stalls for each buck or companion since, even when they play together during the day, bucks get more aggressive in the closer confinement of nighttime quarters. They become downright quarrelsome during breeding season. Mature bucks that are not used to each other will fight, sometimes to the death, and need to be separated by strong fencing.

During breeding season, it takes a well-constructed fence to keep a buck contained. It should either be electrified or six feet high. Prevent bucks from jumping over a lower fence by fitting it with a twelve-inch inward-leaning offset at the top.

To use up excess energy, get needed exercise, and maintain good fertility, bucks need an exercise platform of some sort, or a barrel or other large object to roll around their yard in play.

Chapter 3

DAIRY GOAT RATIONS

There are as many different feeding programs for dairy goats as there are goat herders, ranging from letting the herd forage for most of its sustenance to controlling its entire nutritional intake. Many small-scale keepers combine the two extremes, the amount of integration depending on the quantity of land available, the seasonality of vegetation, and the economic importance of dairy products to the keeper.

Until you get used to your goats and fully understand their needs, you would do well to purchase commercially formulated goat rations and follow the directions on the label, or use the same feeding regimen as a successful herder in your area. Do not use rations designed for other ruminants. Dairy cow feeds may be too high in urea, a protein substitute that can be toxic to goats. Horse rations are too high in fiber.

FUNCTION OF A GOAT'S
FOUR STOMACH CHAMBERS

Rumen   Sometimes called the fermentation vat. The largest chamber, representing about 80 percent of the stomach. Contains micro-organisms (bacteria, protozoa, and fungi) that supply enzymes to break down fiber and convert cellulose into volatile fatty acids, which provide up to 75 percent of the goat's energy needs. Microbes also produce protein from simple nitrogen compounds in the feed, as well as manufacture amino acids and all the vitamin K and B-vitamins a goat needs.

Reticulum Called the honeycomb because that's what it looks like. The second chamber (actually part of the rumen and separated only by a partial wall) functions as a fluid pump. Hardware and other odd objects consumed by a goat remain here and, if sharp or pointed, work their way through the reticulum wall, doing serious damage.

Omasum   Also called many ply because it consists of folds of tissue (like the leaves of a cabbage) for increased surface area and better absorption.

Abomasum The second largest chamber and true stomach, where actual digestion occurs. Contains hydrochloric acid and pepsin enzymes that break down protein into easily digested simple compounds.

FEEDING PRACTICES

Just like their keepers, goats are creatures of habit. They're easily upset by changes in their feeding routine. If you need to alter the diet of your herd, or your established feeding routine, do it gradually over a period of at least ten days and preferably three weeks. This is especially important when you switch them from dry winter hay to fresh spring pasture, when a sudden complete change will cause bloat.

An ideal program approximates as closely as possible the natural habits of goats by feeding small amounts at a time, several times a day, and offering a wide variety of feedstuffs. Variety helps ensure nutritional balance to keep your herd healthy and content.

GOATS AS RUMINANTS

Goats, like sheep, cows, and deer, are classified as ruminants, meaning that their digestive systems consist of four chambers. Digestive problems in goats often result from improper feeding because of the failure of their owners to understand how this system works.

When a ruminant eats, food mixes with saliva and is sent down to the first and largest compartment of the stomach, the *rumen*. A well-developed rumen can hold four or five gallons of liquid and fermenting plant matter. To help fiber break down, soft masses of cud are sent back by the rumen to the mouth for rechewing.

In both the rumen and the second chamber, the *reticulum*, fatty acids and vitamins produced during fermentation are absorbed into the goat's blood stream. In the third and fourth chambers, the *omasum* and *abomasum*, food is further liquified and broken down so that more of its nutrients can be absorbed.

Development of Kids

When a kid is born, the only developed chamber is the abomasum, the true stomach where actual digestion takes place. Kids therefore function essentially as single-stomached animals. As soon as a kid starts eating solid foods, its rumen begins to develop. When the kid chews its cud, all four chambers are functioning, and the animal has become a true ruminant. Its digestive system can then break down fibrous roughage and turn it into a good source of protein—the reason goats are able to survive so well on poor vegetation.

A ruminant requires the proper proportion of roughage to grain in order to maintain good rumen action. Too much grain in relation to roughage is not only unnecessarily costly, but also works against rumen muscle tone. Adult goats whose diets lack adequate fiber lose rumen capacity, and their digestive systems begin to function more like those of single-stomached animals. When too much fiber is fed without the necessary amounts of energy to aid digestion, rumen impaction may result.

Rumen Function

You can tell when a goat's rumen is functioning normally because you can see rhythmic waves of upward movement along the animal's left side, accompanied by frequent unladylike belching and contented cud chewing.

A doe needs good rumen capacity to produce large quantities of milk. But she also needs high quality legume hay, along with a source of energy, to replace nutrients lost in her milk. The result of this low-fiber diet designed for high milk production is that, as lactation progresses, a doe's rumen becomes less active and begins to shrink. Before she starts a new lactation cycle, it is necessary to help her restore rumen function and capacity by feeding her extra amounts of long-fiber, less digestible hay or forage.

ROUGHAGE

Dairy goats need fiber for good rumen action and normal milk fat. They should have it in front of them at all times so they can consume it at a steady rate. Limiting a doe's ability to obtain fiber limits her milk yield. Fiber comes from roughage such as hay, browse, pasture, and crop residues. Goats are browsers by nature and prefer to forage brush-lands or pasture containing a variety of plants. But limited land, type of management, rainfall, and winter weather often preclude natural foraging. In such cases, hay is used as a source of roughage because, when properly stored, it retains its nutritive value quite a long time. Even a herd that has access to natural forage should be fed good hay on a free-choice basis.

Hay quality varies considerably and is influenced by the type of plant grown, weather and other conditions during growth, stage of growth at harvest, whether it comes from a first or subsequent cutting, leaf-to-stem ratio, and conditions of harvest and storage. Legume hay such as alfalfa or clover is the best of the common forages. It is higher in total digestibility and rate of digestion, and is richest is protein, vitamins, and most minerals. Mixed legume-grass hay, if cut early, is also fairly good. Grass hay is generally the poorest quality.

Hay Needs

The type of hay you need depends on the cyclical nutritional needs of your goats. Milkers, for instance, require good legume hay. Too much of a lesser quality fiber will lead to lower milk yield. A dry doe, on the other hand, needs less easily digestible roughage to encourage rumen activity. She'll do better on legume-grass hay, which also better suits her needs in its balance of calcium and phosphorus.

Feed hay free-choice, and add a fresh supply often to keep it from getting dusty or moldy, two conditions that lead to health problems including upset bowels and bloating. Goats tend to scatter and waste hay as they pick it over, so feed only a little at a time, and often. This helps ensure that it's all eaten. Varying the type of hay encourages goats to eat more. How much hay you can expect a goat to eat depends on a variety of factors including age, milking ability, size, and availability of fresh forage. On the average, a goat will consume 2.5 to 3 percent of its own body weight in hay each day.

Hay should be available at all times on a free-choice basis.
(Photo by Matto)

HAY QUALITY EVALUATION

Type	Stage	Possible Score	Your Score
Harvest	Before blossom or heading	26–30	_____
	Early blossom or early heading	21–25	_____
	Mid- to late-bloom, or head	16–20	_____
	Seed stage	11–15	_____
Leafiness	Very leafy	26–30	_____
	Leafy	21–25	_____
	Slightly stemmy	16–20	_____
	Stemmy	11–15	_____
Color	Natural green color of crop	13–15	_____
	Light green	10–12	_____
	Yellow to slightly brown	7– 9	_____
	Brown or black	0– 6	_____
Odor	Clean – "crop odor"	13–15	_____
	Dusty	10–12	_____
	Moldy – mousey or musty	7– 9	_____
	Burnt	0– 6	_____
Softness	Very soft and pliable	9–10	_____
	Soft	7– 8	_____
	Slightly harsh	5– 6	_____
	Harsh, brittle	0– 4	_____
	Subtotal		_____
Penalties	Trash, weeds, dirt, and other foreign material minus	0–35	<_____>
	Total		_____

Scoring	90 and above	– Excellent hay
	80 to 89	– Good hay
	65 to 79	– Fair hay
	Below 65	– Poor hay

From: Joe Burns, et al, Quality Hay Production, Bulletin SR 5004, Alabama Cooperative
Extension Service, Auburn, AL.

Hay Sources and Storage

You can usually buy hay from the grower, at a farmers' cooperative, or in a feed store. For a lot of goats, purchasing hay by the truckload will save you money. If the hay in your area is inferior, trucking it in also gives you access to superior hay from distant areas. If your herd is small, consider joining forces with other goatkeepers or club members to share truckloads. Locate hay markets and growers' cooperatives through the classified ads of commercial farming magazines. Your county Extension agent or state Extension forage specialist may help you locate sellers.

Store hay off the ground and under cover as soon as you get it home. Weathered hay loses both nutrients and digestibility very rapidly. Just a little moisture from dew or a light shower causes rapid loss in quality. A single good rain may cause a 60 percent reduction in food value.

Alternative Forms of Roughage

If you do not have access to good hay, you will have to make up for it with other fibrous feedstuffs. Pelleted hay may be more readily available than baled hay in some areas. Pellets should be large, not the small size commonly fed to rabbits, to ensure adequate fiber length for goats. Pelleted hay is expensive, but goats don't waste it by picking through it, and the higher nutritive value offsets the greater cost by allowing you to reduce supplemental feeding.

Other fibrous feedstuffs include cottonseed hulls, citrus pulp, and beet pulp. Or you can make and store silage during the summer from grass clippings or shredded cornstalks. Sunflower seeds are another excellent source of roughage. They are also high in protein as well as vitamins, minerals, and energy. Of all the types of roughage, though, goats like browse best of all.

BROWSE

Goats were foraging for themselves long before someone got the bright idea to put them into fancy barns and hand-carry all their rations. You will save time and money if you take advantage of their ability and desire to eat coarse weeds and woody growth for at least part of their sustenance. You'll still need to provide hay, but your herd will eat less of it.

Because they pick and choose what they eat, goats are able to satisfy many of their nutritional needs if they can browse a large variety of plants. Woody forage aids rumen development in younger goats and dry does. Milkers enjoy browsing, too, but require supplemental hay and grain for sustained milk yield. If does have to travel far to satisfy their needs, they use up energy that would otherwise go into milk production. In addition, some types of vegetation, especially wild onions and garlic, cause off-flavors in milk. These, along with toxic plants, must be watched for in browse areas. Free-choice access to good quality hay helps keep a herd from seeking out poisonous vegetation. Read more on plant poisoning in chapter 12 on troubleshooting.

PASTURE

Goats are basically browsers like deer, and not grazers like sheep and cattle. But they will make good use of pasture if that's what's available. Free grazing is more common in other countries than it is here in the United States, where we prefer to confine our herds and hand feed them. Yet providing quality pasture is a good way to keep up milk producton while keeping down feed costs. If you have steep, rocky, droughty land that is otherwise unusable, seeding it to pasture will provide grazing for your goats and reduce erosion problems.

You need at least half an acre per animal to minimize parasitic infestations and other unhealthy conditions. Use only well-drained land, or improve the drainage before allowing your herd in. When you pasture

These Nubians relish young pine trees as winter browse. (Photo by Matto)

a herd on lush, green forage, continue free access to hay as a nutritional supplement, and as protection against bloat caused by overloading on greens.

Getting the most forage from your land at the least cost depends on your specific growing conditions including soil type, degree of slope, drainage patterns, fertility and lime levels, plus an entire range of other characteristics that must be taken into consideration. Contact your county Extension agent or Soil Conservation Service conservationist for information about your particular situation.

FORAGE ROTATION

If your goats forage freely, they'll snack on some plants to the exclusion of others, ultimately reducing the forage value of your land. But if you cross-fence, you can let the herd into only one paddock at a time until they have browsed or grazed it down, then rotate them to another. Rotation assures more uniform use of the land and increases the quality and quantity of plant growth, helping further reduce the need for expensive dietary supplements.

Rotation Guidelines

The number of goats that can happily forage on a particular piece of land depends on paddock size, type of vegetation, and how rapidly regrowth takes place given soil fertility, rainfall, and seasonal temperature variations. There are no simple formulas to follow, but there are guidelines that will start you off in the right direction.

Begin with enough land to provide half an acre for each goat. Cross-fence as many times as the terrain, reasonable minimum paddock size for your herd, and your fencing budget allow. The more paddocks you create, the more control you'll have over how long you can let the goats forage in each and how often you need to rotate. For best results, start with at least ten paddocks.

Let the goats forage in the first until brush is browsed down, or the pasture is grazed to about two inches. Then remove the herd until browse regrows six to twelve inches, or pasture reaches six to eight inches. Regrowth will be faster in spring, but slower during hot, dry summer weather. If you have few paddocks and the goats forage too rapidly, let them in for only a short time each day.

During spring, your herd may not be able to keep pasture growth grazed down. In that case take some paddocks out of circulation and mow them to keep plants in the rapid-growth vegetative stage and prevent crowding out of legumes. Use the clippings to make hay or silage for winter feeding. Allow mowed paddocks to rest for twenty-five days and include them back into the rotation scheme by the time they are needed during slower summer regrowth.

Extra spring paddocks may also be used to fatten wethers for meat, or to raise kids away from the adults where they won't pick up worms and other health problems. Rotation is a good health measure in any case, since it keeps a herd from spending too much time in favored areas. Rotation management requires close supervision and constant adjustment, but it's less expensive than buying hay, and less work than growing, baling, and storing it.

CONCENTRATES

In order to produce milk and kids, does need more nutrients than they get from roughage. Concentrates are feed mixtures used to boost nutrition. They're primarily mixed from a variety of grains, which should be whole, rolled, or cracked. Goats don't like finely ground, dusty rations unless they're made palatable by adding a little molasses, which also increases the vitamin content.

Exact nutritional content varies from one concentrate to another, depending on how they're mixed. A dairy goat requires a blend with just the right amount of protein to balance the protein in the type of roughage it eats.

Each goat responds a little differently to concentrates, so you'll have to adjust amounts according to need. The figures you find in books, including this one, are simply averages to give you a starting point. When a goat puts on fat, cut back. Large breeds are too fat when you can't feel the ribs, but if you can't find the ribs of a Pygmy, it's likely muscle that's hiding them. Instead, being able to grab a handful of flesh behind the elbow shows when a Pygmy is too fat.

BALANCING PROTEIN

For	If forage is	Protein required
Lactating does	Legume or mostly legume mix	14–16%
	Grass or mostly grass mix	16–18%
Pregnant dry does	Legume or mostly legume mix	12%
	Grass or mostly grass mix	16%

Based on: Donald L. Ace, Feeding the Dairy Goat, *Special Circular #285, Cooperative Extension Service, The Pennsylvania State University, University Park, PA.*

Feeding Milkers

Lactating does should get about half a pound of concentrate for each pound of milk they give. Those on excellent pasture may not need as much. As you become experienced, you may wish to *challenge feed* your does during the peak of lactation. This involves feeding a little more concentrate each day until the milk yield peaks out. Then gradually decrease the ration as long as the yield remains constant. The amount the doe was eating just before her yield started to drop is exactly what she needs for maximum production without putting on weight. As lactation progresses, a doe's nutritional needs gradually diminish, so cut back on concentrate.

Feeding Dry Does

Non-milking does, called *dry does*, fall into two categories, pregnant ones and non-pregnant ones, or *open does*. An open, dry doe needs no concentrate. To keep her in good flesh without putting on fat, and to ensure proper rumen activity, all she needs is good legume hay or lush legume-grass pasture, or a combination of the two.

Prior to kidding, a pregnant doe needs to be dried off, which is encouraged by decreasing her concentrate. Once a doe is dry, continue feeding the reduced amount until she's close to kidding, unless she requires more because she's very thin, is likely to be carrying more than one kid, or is a heavy milker.

Feeding Schedule

Feed concentrates at two evenly spaced intervals. You may find it convenient to feed milkers at least part of their ration just before or during milking, which helps keep them calm. While some goats practically inhale their feed, others are dainty eaters, so you may have to wait until one is finished before you milk the next. Dry does should be fed in separate stalls or keyhole feeding stations to ensure that each gets a fair share and no more.

Overeating grains causes rapid fermentation in the rumen, leading to serious build-up of gas, a condition called bloat. It is not common where rations are controlled, but occurs if goats are fed when they're very hungry, or if they manage to break into the grain bin and pig out. Seeing that goats get plenty of hay or pasture forage before they eat their concentrate is one way to avoid bloat.

MAINTAINING A BUCK

Good quality hay or pasture available free-choice will keep a buck in good health. Poor hay may cause temporary or permanent sterility. If your buck is getting lots of exercise, as he should, he may need supplemental energy from the same concentrate you feed your does. Adjust his grain intake as necessary to maintain his body weight without putting on fat.

During the breeding season, feed a large buck around two pounds of concentrate a day, and a Pygmy about one pound. Depending on his condition and amount of activity, a good stud buck may need considerably more concentrate during the height of the breeding season. Weight loss during that time is normal. Your concern is to guard against undesirable weight gain that will affect breeding ability and fertility.

Chapter 4

NUTRITIONAL
NEEDS

As you gain experience, you may begin to develop your own ideas on customizing rations. In order to do that, you must identify the nutritional needs of your goats and establish feeding goals based on a clear understanding of the nutrient values and functions of each type of feedstuff. Only then will you be ready to combine those that satisfy your needs and goals at the best possible price. Since feed costs represent some 40 to 50 percent of a herd's upkeep, it makes good sense to look for ways to reduce the cost without endangering nutrition. Mixing feeds for proper balance requires a comprehensive chart tabulating the nutrient content of each. Sources for such charts are listed at the back of this book.

Formulating rations for maximum milk production at the lowest cost is both a science and an art. It is easiest done with the aid of computer software designed for ration balancing. But with a thorough understanding of the principles of dairy goat nutrition, you can do a reasonable job without computer assistance. The result will be good health for your herd, high milk production, and a strong, vigorous annual crop of kids.

ESSENTIAL NUTRIENTS

A doe's nutritional needs change with her stage of maturity, level of activity, and whether she's in early or late pregnancy, or early or late lactation. Does in late pregnancy and early lactation, for instance, have much heavier nutritional needs than non-pregnant dry does. Similarly, during breeding season, bucks have greater needs than at other times of the year. Important nutrients for all goats are energy—expressed either as total digestible nutrients (TDN) or estimated net energy (ENE) —protein, minerals, vitamins, and water.

Energy

Carbohydrates and fats together provide dietary energy, which influences growth, the onset of puberty, fertility and normal reproduction, lactation, and resistance to diseases and parasites. A goat's exact needs depend on its age, size, stage of growth, degree of activity, weather conditions, stress, and the balance of other dietary elements.

NUTRITIONAL COMPOSITION OF THREE POPULAR CONCENTRATE CONSTITUENTS

Contents (dry basis)	Sunflower seeds	Corn	Oats
Crude Protein	17.9%	10.9%	13.6%
Crude Fiber	31.0	2.4	12.2
Energy: Fats	27.7	4.5	5.6
Carbohydrates	20.1	80.8	56.2
Minerals	3.3	1.4	3.4
Total Digestible Nutrients	82.0	93.0	77.0

From: George F. Haenlein, "Feeding Sunflowers Can Prevent Enterotoxemia." Feedstuffs, August 2, 1982: 23.

A newborn kid may be weak if its mother received too little nutritional energy. Insufficient energy may delay a doe's first heat. For a milker to be a top producer and maintain her body weight, she needs sufficient quantities of energy. High yield milkers and does carrying several kids tend to overeat if their rations are low in energy. Excess energy, on the other hand, causes the accumulation of body fat and can inhibit conception, endanger a doe's health during kidding, and over-condition a show animal.

Deficiency is most likely to occur during the early stages of lactation. A good milk producer needs as much as 5 percent of her body weight in energy each day.

Protein

Protein is the primary constituent of every cell in the bodies of all living animals. Protein is essential for growth, general maintenance, disease resistance, reproduction, and lactation. For goats, protein quality —its amino acid content— is not an important consideration except in the diet of high-yield milkers. As long as a goat gets enough dietary protein, it is able to synthesize the essential amino acids in its digestive system. A doe needs .07 pound of protein for each pound of milk she gives that's 4 percent in butterfat.

Protein deficiency may lead to delay in puberty and heat, as well as cause pregnancy problems. Excess protein is either eliminated by the kidneys or burned off as energy, making it an unnecessary expense to feed more protein than your herd needs.

VITAMINS

To date, the vitamin requirements of goats have not been thoroughly researched. It is known that their needs are relatively small, and it is believed that if they are allowed to forage, they easily obtain all the vitamins they require. Stall-fed dairy goats, especially high-yield milkers, may need a supplement of vitamins A, D, and E. Vitamins C and K and the B vitamins, are all manufactured within a goat's body.

Goats need vitamin A for tissue growth and maintenance, good reproductive abilities, and resistance to diseases. Vitamin A keeps udder cells healthy and less susceptible to infection. Deficiency in kids causes watery eyes, respiratory problems, and nasal discharge. Coughing and diarrhea may also occur, culminating in pneumonia. Older goats may become more susceptible to infection, or become night-blind so that they panic when you approach them in the dark. Deficiency may also cause temporary or permanent infertility in bucks. A goat's digestive system produces vitamin A from its precursor, carotene, which exists in yellow corn, carrots, and green forage but is deficient in old and weathered hay.

Vitamin D is essential for proper absorption of calcium and phosphorus. Since it is synthesized on the skin of goats, plenty of sunshine is usually all they need to obtain adequate quantities.

Vitamin E is important to milk quality and storability, and to reproduction. It is contained in most fresh feeds, but oxidizes rapidly so that old hay and ground grains become poor sources.

Vitamin deficiencies, like all nutritional problems, are hard to identify because of the complex interrelationship of vitamins with other nutrients, and because deficiency of only one vitamin is rare. Identification of a deficiency requires laboratory analysis of a goat's hair or blood. Luckily, goats store vitamins in their bodies during the summer to help carry them through the winter. As a precaution, you might include pelleted alfalfa in the winter rations, or add 300,000 units of commercially prepared A, D, and E to each 100 pounds of concentrate.

COMPLETE DAIRY RATION

Feed	% TDN
Crude protein	14%
Digestible protein	11%
Total digestible nutrients	63–64%
Fiber	16–18%
Calcium	.6– 1%
Phosphorus	.4–.5%
Vitamin A	6–10 million units
Mineralized salt	.5– 1%

Dietary intake varies with the animal's condition and level of production.

From: Barney Harris, Jr., et al, Dairy Goat Production Guide, Circular #452, Cooperative Extension Agency, University of Florida, Gainesville, FL.

MINERALS

As with vitamins, the exact mineral requirements of goats have not been determined. It is known that they need relatively large quantities of seven major elements—calcium, phosphorus, magnesium, sodium, chlorine, potassium, and sulfur. Many other trace elements are needed in lesser amounts. Deficiencies lead to reproductive problems and may influence the sex ratio of kids. Most likely to suffer deficiencies are very high or very low milk producers. Heavy milkers may not be able to keep up with their needs solely through their rations, and low producers may eat too little to fulfill their nutritional needs. The proportion of one mineral to another is just as important as the amount of each in the diet.

Trace minerals are usually adequate if you use a reputable commercial dairy ration or supply a variety of feedstuffs obtained from different sources, and especially if rations include alfalfa hay, legume pasture, or quality browse. Free-choice mineralized salt should round out your herd's mineral needs. Nutritional supplements are available, but should be used selectively. Going overboard is a waste of money.

Calcium

Calcium is necessary for growth and bone development. Milk is high in calcium, so the more milk a doe gives, the more calcium she needs. On the average she should get about .022 ounces per pound of 4 percent milk. Deficiency leads to reduced milk production. Feed-grade limestone is a relatively inexpensive calcium supplement. Alfalfa is also a good source, but grass or mixed hay and pasture are not.

Phosphorus

Calcium and phosphorus are interrelated and should appear in rations in the proportion of 2 to 1. Phosphorus is needed for tissue growth and bone development, and is important for its ability to trap energy during digestion. Silage and good grain mixtures usually contain sufficient quantities of phosphorus.

Magnesium

Magnesium influences proper functioning of the nervous system, and is related to the need for both calcium and phosphorus. Magnesium deficiency occurs in regions that are naturally low in this mineral. If you pasture goats on small grains or grasses in an area where grass

CLINICAL SIGNS OF DIETARY DEFICIENCIES

	Slow Growth	Reduced Appetite	Impaired Reproduction	Weak Offspring	Lowered Milk	Other Effects
Energy	x		x		x	Reduced condition
Protein	x	x	x	x	x	Poor feed efficiency
Calcium	x	x	x	x	x	Milk fever
Phosphorus	x	x	x	x	x	Milk fever, poor feed efficiency
Magnesium	x	x	x	x		Tetany, milk fever
Selenium	x		x			White muscle disease
Potassium	x	x			x	Poor consumption
Sulfur		x	x			Weakness, dullness
Salt	x	x		x	x	Rough coat
Copper	x					Anemia
Iron	x	x	x			Anemia
Cobalt	x					Anemia
Zinc	x	x			x	Dermatosis
Manganese	x		x	x		Irregular estrus
Iodine			x	x		Goiter

From: Barney Harris, Jr., et al, Dairy Goat Production Guide, Circular #452, Cooperative Extension Agency, University of Florida, Gainesville, FL.

tetany affects cattle, feed them alfalfa hay or add a magnesium supplement such as magnesium oxide. Loss of appetite and excitability leading to convulsions are possible symptoms of deficiency.

Sodium and Chlorine

Salt, or sodium-chloride, is the mineral compound most likely to be lacking in a goat's diet, since a doe may lose as much as one ounce of salt for every gallon of milk she produces. Mineralized salt should be available on a free-choice basis in loose form. Goats cannot lick enough salt from a block to satisfy their needs. Sodium deficiency is indicated by the eating of soil, poor coat, and heat stress.

Sodium bicarbonate

The compound sodium bicarbonate, or baking soda, is necessary to maintain proper rumen pH for maximum absorption of essential nutrients and for the prevention of digestive disorders such as acidosis. Like loose salt, baking soda should be available on a free-choice basis.

Potassium

Potassium is required in relatively large amounts, but is rarely lacking in roughage-based rations. Deficiency occurs primarily in diets that are heavy in either grains or weathered hay.

Sulfur

Sulfur is a component of all body protein and is contained in sufficient amounts in most feeds, though it may be low in feedstuffs grown in deficient soils. Check with your county Extension agent or a local livestock veterinarian to find out if you need to be concerned about a deficiency in your area.

Iodine

The important trace mineral iodine is also lacking in some parts of the country, requiring the use of an iodized salt mix to prevent goiter, the enlargement of the thyroid gland. Deficiency may cause weak or dead kids. Excess dietery iodine is secreted in the milk.

Selenium

In some regions of the United States, natural selenium from the soil appears in hay and grain in levels that are toxic to goats, causing anemia, staggering, blindness, paralysis, and sometimes death. On the other hand, in many parts of the country—notably the East Coast, the Great Lakes region, New England, Florida, and the Northeast—soils are deficient in selenium. In those areas, supplementation of this trace mineral is necessary when goats are fed only locally grown rations.

Deficiency has been linked to white muscle disease (muscular dystrophy) and certain reproductive problems. Sudden death in kids under two weeks old, and stiffness in the hind legs of older kids, may also occur. A good source of selenium is brewer's grain. Where deficiency is a serious threat, selenium injections are necessary.

WATER

Goats are considered on a par with camels in the efficient use of water. They get along better than any other dairy animal with little of it, but a doe cannot sustain milk production without sufficient water to replace lost body fluids. In fact, water—specifically, water quality and quantity—probably affects milk production more than any single nutrient. Yet of the essential dietary elements, water is overlooked the most often.

By weight, a goat's body is more than 60 percent water. Water is lost not only in milk, but also through urination, perspiration, and evaporation. If a goat is unable to drink enough, it will eat less, even to the point of starvation. Since milk contains 87 percent water, a doe that persists as a high producer without enough to drink will suffer from dehydration. When a goat loses 20 percent or more of its body water, it dies.

Water Quality

Goats may refuse water into which manure or other debris has fallen. For that reason, water for dairy goats must be clean and pure, particularly during warm weather when their needs increase. It's good practice to change drinking water at least twice a day and clean containers often, especially if algae or scum tend to develop. Water containers may be kept sparkling with a good dairy disinfectant, used according to directions on the label.

Adding molasses to the rations causes does to drink more, leading to increased milk production. Offering cool water in the summer and warm water in winter also encourages drinking. Never force goats to eat snow, either because you fail to keep them supplied with water or because the water becomes frozen and inaccessible. During winter months, if you furnish dry does and bucks enough warm water for them to drink their fill, you need water only once a day.

Water helps control body temperature, improves digestion and assimilation of nutrients, and aids the elimination of body wastes. Factors that influence a goat's water needs include environmental temperature, exercise, moisture content of forage, dietary salt and other minerals, and milk yield. A lactating doe needs more to drink than the amount of milk she gives. Ready access to free-choice water for milkers improves milk yield by more than 10 percent over the common practice of watering twice a day. If possible, install automatic watering devices to ensure a continuous supply of fresh, pure water to keep your milk pail full.

SAMPLE CONCENTRATES

Desired protein content	14%	16%	18%
Corn	37*	35*	32*
Oats	37	35	32
Wheat bran	16	14	15
Soy or linseed oil meal	9	15	20
Dicalcium phosphate	.5	.5	.5
Trace mineral salt	.5	.5	.5
Total	100%	100%	100%

*Percentage of total ration.

From: National Research Council, Nutrient Requirements of Domestic Animals #15 – Nutrient Requirements of Goats. National Academy Press, 1981.

(Photo by Matto)

Chapter 5

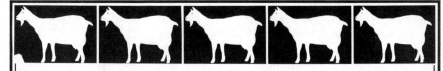

DAIRY GOAT MANAGEMENT

When goats know what you expect of them, they happily comply, so it pays to keep a regular schedule. It also helps to understand a little goat psychology. Like other social animals, goats establish a pecking order. If you keep this in mind in all your management procedures, you'll have fewer problems. For instance, feed and milk the dominant goats first to minimize squabbles.

Every herd is led by a herd boss. It may be a buck or a wether, but in most cases it's the oldest and most experienced doe, called the herd queen. The other animals are reluctant to move until she leads the way. Training your herd is easier if you concentrate on seeing that the leader is well-mannered and cooperative.

Avoiding Stress

Gentle handling is the key to success in all phases of management. Whenever you milk, groom, feed, medicate, or perform any other procedure, talk to your goats. Use the name of each so it develops a sense of reassurance from the sound. After any particularly unpleasant experience, keep talking calmly until you have the animal settled in its usual quarters.

Gentleness and patience on your part help reduce stress. Minimizing stress improves productivity as well as your herd's ability to withstand disease. Common stressful situations are weaning, castration, disbudding, transporting, isolation, artificial insemination, surgery, and any unusual, painful, or unpleasant procedure including rough handling during otherwise unstressful situations.

Whenever possible, precondition your goats to each new procedure. Take a first freshener to the milk stand regularly to get her used to the idea before you actually start milking her. Giving every member of your herd a regular periodic health check makes it easier to slip in the occasional vaccination or booster shot.

Overregimentation can also lead to stress, so it pays to vary your routine somewhat. For instance, have family members share your goat-keeping chores to reduce stress whenever someone else has to take over for you.

Doelings with frequent human contact from birth are less likely to be stressed later, when they're handled during kidding and milking. If you acquire a goat that's wild and skittish through lack of human contact, let it get used to you without feeling threatened. Instead of approaching the animal, which may cause it to panic and run, stand still or kneel down and let it check you out. Goats allowed to set their own pace when investigating anything new are less likely to be stressed than those forced to confront the situation.

Goats Love Attention

Goats are normally friendly and thrive on attention. They love to be petted and rubbed, but don't like having their ears or tails pulled, even in play. Never let a goat, even a little one, jump on you or butt, and never wrestle with a horned goat. It all seems such fun until the day an overly playful animal, or one that's a bit cranky, gets carried away and causes serious damage.

Don't be concerned if the animals in your herd are not textbook examples. There's no such thing as a "normal" goat. Like each herder, each goat is an individual with its own special patterns and quirks—and that's perfectly normal.

HANDLING AND TRANSPORTING

Friendly, well-trained goats that are used to your routine can be caught and managed by voice command. Young animals, and new ones in your herd, may test your patience. Have collars on each to make them easier to handle—for example, when you want to let one goat out and others try to follow, or when you let one back in and others decide to go out. Holding a goat by its collar gives you better control. The best type of collar is made from a special chain that breaks if it gets hung up. It's the only kind to use for goats that browse and may easily get caught in brush.

A goat that isn't quite used to you, and does not have a collar, should be grabbed under the chin. A bearded goat has a handy handle for the purpose. If the animal dances around, tip its head upward to catch it off balance. If you're leading a goat that tries to bolt, put one hand under its jaw and pull back to bring it to a standstill. Then start out again. Hang onto a rambunctious buck with one hand on his collar and the other on one ear.

A goat is best restrained by confining its head in a stanchion like the one at the head of a milk stand, but you can also use a halter tied securely to a post. When you milk, check an injury, or perform any other procedure on a jumpy animal, press against its flank with your head or arm while you work. A goat that persists in prancing around is only testing your endurance. Don't give in and it will give up.

Transporting goats causes a lot of stress, especially because it often requires them to be in drafty conditions. Pneumonia may result, sometimes accompanied by diarrhea—a condition called *shipping fever*. Always transport goats with protection against the cold and wet, and with proper ventilation during hot weather. Some folks travel with their goats in the family car, with or without the back seat removed. In such cases, don't let the animal stick its head out the window, as goats so love to do. Wind and flying insects too easily cause eye injury.

Providing all the comforts, especially if you have an appreciable distance to go, reduces stress. Take along a rack of hay as something familiar to munch, and stop twice a day for exercise and water. When goats travel often they get used to it. Show goats learn to anticipate all the attention they'll get in the showroom, and look forward to the outings.

CLEANLINESS

Dairy goats like to be kept clean. They also produce better, remain healthier, and are less apt to offend you or your neighbors if you help them stay that way. Start by providing a thick layer of dry bedding. It can be straw, leaves, peanut hulls, or any other absorbent material you can get at a good price. A thick layer will prevent bruised knees, and keep udders off the cold, dirty floor. Goats like to lie with their heads uphill, so if you don't have sloped sleeping platforms, provide extra bedding where they normally put their heads.

Watch for damp spots in the bedding caused by leaky roofs and walls, or drippy waterers. Repair the condition causing the dampness, and replace all damp or moldy bedding. Add fresh bedding as often as necessary, or remove manure. Don't let manure build up on top of the bedding, where it will release too much moisture. Once a year, or more often if conditions warrant, thoroughly clean out the shelter. Clean-up and disinfection are essential after any successful treatment for a contagious or infectious disease.

Cleaning the Shelter

Choose a warm, sunny day so you can keep the herd outside while you work, and so the facilities will dry quickly when you're through. Using a garden hose attachment, lightly spray the housing with a disinfectant to settle the dust. Remove and clean all equipment and movable fixtures. Clean out all bedding. Scrape away dirt accumulations. Brush down the walls with a stout brush or an old broom. With the same brush or broom, scrub the entire inside of the building with boiling water. A little detergent or household bleach will increase its cleansing power. After a disease outbreak, follow up with a dairy disinfectant or one recommended by your vet. Air out and dry housing completely before replacing the bedding and letting the herd back in.

What time of year should you schedule annual cleanup? Some do it in the fall, on the grounds that their goats spend more time indoors during cold weather and so their shelter should start out clean. Others leave the bedding and manure pack to provide heat during winter months, cleaning up in spring when fresh bedding creates cooler conditions. Both arguments have merit. Do what works best for you.

GROOMING

Goats enjoy a brisk daily brushing with a coarse kitchen brush. It keeps their coats smooth and discourages lice. If you brush each doe just before milking, there's less chance that loose hair and other debris will fall into the milk pail. Clipping the hair from the udder, belly, and flanks also helps keep does clean, and prevents uncomfortable hair-pulling during milking. If you trim the hair when the udder is full, the job will be easier. In late spring, clipping all long hair keeps goats cooler, puts them in good condition for show, and reduces buck odor. A variety of electrical clippers is available from many of the supply outlets listed at the back of this book.

Occasional dirt stains can be washed away with warm water and a baby shampoo or a mild shampoo sold for use on livestock. Apply the sudsy water with a brush. Over-all washing may be difficult since most goats dislike water, but it is possible with the aid of a livestock wash rack like those at many fairgrounds. A smelly buck will benefit from a bath on a warm day. Follow up baths or spot-washes with a rinse, then dry completely and let the animal out in the warm sunlight to prevent chilling.

TRADITIONAL HAIR STYLES

Style	Purpose	Procedure
DAIRY CLIP	Keep hair and dirt out of milk; prevent hair-pulling during milking.	Clip very short on udder, flanks, thighs, tail, and back part of belly. Remove beard.
BUCK CLIP	Improve breeding; reduce odor.	Clip belly, scrotum area, penis sheath. Remove beard if it develops bad odor.
WINTER CLIP	Neatness; show conditioning.	Trim head, tail, lower legs, and belly, blending smoothly into unclipped area. Trim shaggy forelegs of bucks if hair ices up from urination.
SUMMER CLIP	Coolness; show conditioning.	Dark goats—trim entire coat. Light goats—trim face, belly, legs, tail, and shaggy areas.

Hold clipper-head flat to the body and use long, smooth strokes against the natural direction of hair growth.

HOOF TRIMMING

Goats evolved with fast-growing hooves to compensate for the wearing action of sand and rocks in their natural habitat, and the rate of growth has not decreased with domestication. Part of good grooming is to keep your goats' hooves neatly trimmed.

The hoof has a thin outer wall of *keratin*, the same material fingernails are made of. This keratin layer surrounds the firm, fleshy cushion of the sole, or *frog*. When the keratin grows beyond the frog, it folds over, collects manure and moisture, and becomes subject to infections such as hoof rot. The hoof begins to twist. The goat cannot walk properly, experiences pain, and eventually becomes permanently deformed.

To learn how a healthy hoof looks, study the feet of a kid.
(Photo by Matto)

Proper Procedure

Check hooves as part of your grooming sessions. How often they'll need trimming varies with each animal, the amount of exercise it gets, the type of ground it's kept on, and even what it eats. A properly trimmed hoof is flat on the bottom and has a boxy look. The keratin layer and frog are of even thickness, front to back, and the toes are equal in length. The best way to learn what a proper hoof looks like is to examine the feet of a newborn kid.

Hooves that have been softened by the moisture of rain or dewy grass are easier to trim. Put the goat up on the milk stand. Have a sharp jackknife, good garden pruning shears, or hoof trimmers ready, along with a rasp, file, or hoof plane.

Grasp one ankle and bend the hoof back, placing it over your knee for control. Scrape away accumulated dirt with the point of your trimming tool. Cut off long toes. Cut bent-over parts of the keratin layer parallel to the visible growth rings. When the outer hoof is even with the frog, smooth down the frog's white cushion by taking a tiny slice at a time. Cut from the heel toward the toe. Stop trimming when the white part shows the slightest sign of pink, since you're getting close to the foot's blood supply.

A goat unused to the procedure may struggle a bit, but that's not because you're hurting it. More likely, the animal does not like standing on three legs. Serious injury during hoof trimming is unlikely if you work slowly and have good light so you can see what you're doing. Once the hoof is in pretty good shape, flatten and finish it with the plane or file. If you trim hooves often enough, this will be the only tool you'll need.

Trim the hooves of a doe early in pregnancy and then don't do it again until after she kids. A pregnant doe that objects to trimming because it makes her uncomfortable may kick too hard and lose her kids. Be sure your buck's hooves are well trimmed prior to the breeding season.

WEIGHING

There are times when you'll want to weigh your goats, such as to track the growth of kids, determine if a doe is old enough to breed, check for any unusual weight gain or loss, and estimate how much meat is on a wether or a cull doe. Few herders feel it's worth purchasing an expensive livestock platform scale. There are other ways to determine a goat's weight. Lighter animals can be held and weighed on a bathroom scale. Those up to to fifty pounds may be hung from a sling on the milk scale.

For larger goats, weighing tapes convert heart girth into an estimate of weight. Or use any flexible dressmaker's tape measure and the accompanying conversion chart. Place the tape snugly around the barrel, just behind the front legs. Then convert the measurement into an estimate of the goat's weight. If you record this estimate and the date on each goat's data sheet, it will help you track unusual changes that may signal nutritional or disease problems.

ESTIMATING WEIGHT

Heart Girth	Weight	Heart Girth	Weight	Heart Girth	Weight
10.25"	4.5#	21.25"	35#	32.25"	101#
10.75	5	21.75	37	32.75	105
11.25	5.5	22.25	39	33.25	110
11.75	6	22.75	42	33.75	115
12.25	6.5	23.25	45	34.25	120
12.75	7	23.75	48	34.75	125
13.25	8	24.25	51	35.25	130
13.75	9	24.75	54	35.75	135
14.25	10	25.25	57	36.25	140
14.75	11	25.75	60	36.75	145
15.25	12	26.25	63	37.25	150
15.75	13	26.75	66	37.75	155
16.25	15	27.25	69	38.25	160
16.75	17	27.75	72	38.75	165
17.25	19	28.25	75	39.25	170
17.75	21	28.75	78	39.75	175
18.25	23	29.25	81	40.25	180
18.75	25	29.75	84	40.75	185
19.25	27	30.25	87	41.25	190
19.75	29	30.75	90	41.75	195
20.25	31	31.25	93	42.25	200
20.75	33	31.75	97		

DEHORNING

Horns add to a goat's character. The horns of the Swiss breeds grow upright and sickle shaped, while those of other breeds tend to grow sideways and sometimes spiral. Along with hooves, horns are a goat's defense against predators.

But horns have no place in a dairy herd. They interfere with the use of keyhole stanchions. They allow a goat to get hung up in fences that often must be cut to release the animal. Even the gentlest doe is unaware that her horns can cause serious injury if she turns her head in the wrong place at the wrong time. She may wound other goats during play or during squabbles that lead to serious butting sessions. Horned bucks are even more dangerous because they like to show off their virility, and horns on a belligerent buck are downright lethal. In addition to all this, horns on any goat but a Pygmy are grounds for disqualification from a show.

Horns have no place in a dairy herd, and are grounds for disqualification of all breeds except Pygmy.

Some goats are naturally hornless, a condition called *polled*, that has nothing to do with the breed but with family line. All others should have their hornbuds removed early through a procedured called *disbudding*, in which horn cells are destroyed to prevent horns from growing. It's a relatively simple process you can do yourself, following the directions in chapter 8. But some goat herders either neglect to disbud their kids, or else deliberately take their chances with horned goats because they like the natural look. If you're interested in acquiring an animal and it still has its horns, have them removed before including the animal in your herd. Horn removal may also be necessary where improper disbudding has resulted in the growth of misshapen horns, called *scurs*.

Dehorning is quite a traumatic surgical operation, requiring removal of about half of an inch of skin along with the horns. It is best done by a veterinarian or a very experienced goatkeeper.

Surgical dehorning is required when a scur curls back into an animal's neck or face. (Photo by Matto)

MANAGEMENT REMINDERS

SUMMER   Ensure good air circulation by opening windows. Provide shade, salt, and fresh, cool water. Avoid overcrowding. During hot weather, cut back on high energy feeds and watch for overgrazing of forage.

FALL   Clean out barn and stalls or add a fresh thick layer of absorbent bedding. Keep accurate estrus and breeding records.

WINTER   Provide warm drinking water. Guard against damp bedding. Watch for drafts or moisture in closed housing. Increase energy feeds during cold weather.

SPRING   Check fences and gates for winter damage. Guard against bloat from lush pasture. Plan ahead for kidding. Clean and disinfect housing if not done in fall.

ALL TIMES   Trim hooves as often as necessary. Keep coats brushed and clean. Clip shaggy coats, hair on bellies and udders of does, and belly hair of bucks.

DE-SCENTING BUCKS

Well-groomed, properly managed bucks should not develop offensive odors. Keeping the hair clipped from a buck's belly and forelegs, and making sure his housing and yard stay neat and clean, are just as important as similar care for his ladies. If a buck's odor still bothers you, you can have his scent glands removed.

Odor comes from musk glands on a buck's legs near his tail, and on his head along the sides of an imaginary V connecting his hornbuds to the cowlick. The smell is strongest during breeding season, and can be used to detect does in heat. But the ladies find a buck just as attractive without his odor, and de-scenting has no effect on his breeding abilities.

De-scenting involves only the glands on the head, so some small amount of less powerful odor will still be produced by the leg glands. De-scenting is usually done at the time of disbudding, but you can have the glands of a mature animal surgically removed by a vet. It is not a complicated operation, and when it heals, the buck's head will look just as neat as before.

Chapter 6

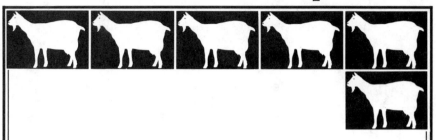

CHOOSING DAMS AND SIRES

If you keep only a few family milk goats, chances are you won't be too interested in the intricacies of selective breeding, except to the extent that you may strive to receive top dollar for the kids you sell. On the other hand, if you intend to build up a sizable herd, careful selective breeding will increase its value. The two basic rules of selective breeding are:

- **Never mate two goats that have the same fault, no matter how minor it seems.**
- **Keep sight of your goals, and make every decision with those goals in mind.**

Goals may include improving milk production, increasing the kidding rate, or decreasing susceptibility to certain health conditions.

Breeding for appearance alone often leads to degeneration of milk qualities or reproductive capabilities. Whatever else your goals, include among them traits involving good dairy character. Any time you get close to achieving your goals, raise your standards.

Selective Breeding

Selection in favor of desirable characteristics involves culling against undesirable ones. Unwanted hereditary defects include overshot or undershot jaw, anomalies of the teeth or joints, extra or double teats, an undescended testicle, weak anatomical structure, or incorrect conformation and color for the breed.

How fast you make progress toward your goals depends on the accuracy of your records, how good your foundation stock is, the uniformity of its gene pool, the number of breeders you select from, the relationship between the traits you're selecting for, and their degree of heritability. Fortunately, most of the desirable traits for dairy goats are heritable to a fairly high degree. Some traits are not genetically controlled but depend on environment, nutrition, and other factors. You can reach your goals faster if you concentrate on only one trait at a time, but if you ignore all others, undesirable ones may creep in.

Don't be fooled by exciting, early success, which may give you a false sense of satisfaction about your selection abilities. This is especially so if you start out with unrelated goats so that your first few matings produce exceptionally fine kids, the result of hybrid vigor. Only years of careful selection can make you certain of the pedigree of each goat in your breeding team, and sure that no undesirable latent characteristics lurk in the background. Selective breeding takes lots of record keeping, and lots of patience.

Inbreeding

Methods of selective breeding include inbreeding, linebreeding, outbreeding, and crossbreeding. Inbreeding is the mating of closely related animals to develop a uniform genetic base so that eventually every goat in your herd is nearly identical in production and/or appearance. Inbreeding allows this by intensifying desirable characteristics, but it can also intensify undesirable ones if they are not carefully culled against. One of the benefits of inbreeding is precisely that it brings out latent weaknesses to make you aware that they exist, so you can work toward eliminating them. If, after four or five generations of inbreeding, you continue to produce sound offspring, you can be pretty sure there are no hidden genetic defects in your herd.

Linebreeding

Linebreeding is a form of inbreeding. Its purpose is to concentrate the blood of one founding parent, usually a buck but it may also be a doe. Many books contain linebreeding charts, which should be considered little more than suggested guidelines. There's simply no way to predict the final results of a breeding program based on some predetermined formula. Blindly plugging the names of goats into a chart just because of their position in the family tree is likely to produce only frustration and disappointment. Instead, choose each breeder according to its individual merit and its potential for bringing you closer to your goals.

The effectiveness of any form of inbreeding is increased with the number of goats involved, which may be divided among cooperating herders. A large breeding population lets you cull ruthlessly to keep only animals that bring you closer to your goals. Because it requires such heavy culling, inbreeding is not viable for very small herds.

Outbreeding

Outbreeding is the opposite of inbreeding. It involves mating animals that are not closely related or are entirely unrelated. Its goal is to combine the desirable traits of two distinct populations, with the additional advantage that it produces hybrid vigor, a phenomenon in which the offspring have traits that make them superior to either parent.

Outbreeding becomes necessary in an inbreeding program when undesirable traits pop up, or when it turns out that a herd can't be developed according to plan because it doesn't carry the genetics for certain desired characteristics. Outbreeding involves careful selection of an animal to complement your herd, with the particular characteristics you need and no undesirable ones that will throw your program out of kilter. Such a goat is most likely to be found in another herd that is linebred, preferably one with distant ancestors common to your herd.

Crossbreeding

Crossbreeding is a form of outbreeding in which animals of different breeds are mated. It is done by trained researchers for experimental purposes, by some commercial dairy owners interested only in milk production, and by amateurs who delight in seeing what turns out. Crossbreeding is so common in backyard herds that names have evolved for the resulting offspring—Nutog for a Nubian–Toggenburg cross, for instance, and Pygnu for a Pygmy–Nubian cross.

DEGREE OF HERITABILITY OF
CERTAIN TRAITS

Trait	Heritability (%)
Milk:	
Total yield	25–60
Fat yield	30–47
Fat, %	32–62
Protein yield	32–47
Protein, %	59
Casein, %	65
Lactose, %	38
Flavor	27
Milking speed	67
Birth weight	1
Live weight at 7 months	49–77
General body weight	50
Age at first kidding	54–77
Number of kids	10

Exact degree of heritability is not easy to ascertain due to the interrelationship of heritable characteristics as well as the complications of undetected environmental and nutritional factors. Estimates of heritability show the percentage of progress you can reasonably expect when breeding selected parents. They help in making trade-off decisions when breeding for more than one trait.

Compiled from: George F. W. Haenlein, "Inheritance of Type and Milk Production in Goats," in Sheep and Goat Handbook, *Vol. 4, Westview Press, 1984; and Maurice Shelton, "Reproduction and Breeding of Goats," Journal of Dairy Science, 61:994–1010, 1978.*

EVALUATING BREEDERS

There are several ways to evaluate the worthiness of potential breeders. One is to look at showroom experience. If you want to breed for winners, it helps to mate winners. But show wins are often weighted in favor of appearance over dairy character. In addition, showroom placement is determined by comparing the exhibited animals to each other, rather than to some ideal.

A second means of evaluation is through classification, a system of scoring by comparing each goat to an established standard of excellence for its breed. Classifiers are trained and licensed by the various dairy goat registries. Like showroom scoring, classification involves some degree of subjectivity on the part of the judge.

A third alternative that provides more objective evaluation is linear appraisal. The system was established by a committee within the National Association of Animal Breeders as a means of placing value on individual traits by using a sliding scale from worst to best. It was designed to evaluate bulls used for artificial insemination. As of this writing, its use for dairy goats has not yet been fully exploited.

Progeny Testing

Perhaps the most objective way to analyze breeders is through progeny testing, which involves keeping track of an animal's offspring. The USDA Dairy Herd Improvement Association (DHIA) sponsors a progeny testing program to identify superior breeders. One of the main values of the system is that it uses specialized methods to distinguish between genetic and environmental considerations. Participation is voluntary and fees are charged. Enrollment through one of the dairy goat registries allows official recognition on the papers of superior animals. Even if you don't enroll your herd, you can use the published data to make decisions when purchasing stock or choosing a buck to mate with your does through artificial insemination.

Since each genetic trait is influenced by thousands of genes, there is no way to know precisely the outcome of any particular mating. But offspring should be better than their dam if she is bred to a top quality, proven buck.

It has also been shown that a superior buck influences the milk production of the does to whom he is mated. This is possible because among the stimuli for milk production are certain hormones produced during gestation by the fetal-placental unit. A fetus with higher genetic potential than its dam can therefore increase its mother's milking abilities and influence her udder development. This has been used to improve the milking abilities of Pygmies. It pays to mate your does to the best buck you can find, even when you don't plan to keep the kids.

Progeny testing helps to identify superior bucks like this handsome Toggenburg.
(Photo by Matto)

HEAT CYCLES

Goats have a breeding season during which does come into heat for a day or two every few weeks. The Swiss breeds, with origins far from the equator, are short daylight breeders. They come into season during the fall and early winter from about mid-September through December. Nubians and Pygmies, having originated closer to the equator, are less seasonal and may come into heat at other times, too. A buck's sexuality is just as affected by season as a doe's.

Each doe comes into heat every seventeen to twenty-three days until she is successfully bred or the temperature and daylight length begin to increase. Heat lasts anywhere from a few hours to three days, with about eighteen hours being average. Each doe develops her own repeating pattern, so accurate records for every doe in your herd—when heat starts, how long it lasts, and how much time lapses between heat periods—will improve your breeding success.

Manipulating Estrus

You can influence the occurrence of heat, which offers advantages if you have quite a few does. Manipulating heat cycles helps produce a more regular flow of milk from your herd by allowing groups of does to freshen at the times you designate, even at times of year other than normally allowed by the regular breeding season. Synchronizing heat —having does come into heat together—makes artificial insemination cheaper and easier, condenses the period during which you have to be on hand for kidding, and produces groups of kids of similar ages that can be more easily raised together. A disadvantage is that conception rates and fetus survival rates tend to be lower during out-of-season hot summer months.

Estrus—the technical word for heat—may be controlled in four basic ways. Two involve hormonal treatment and are not very practical for the average herder. The third is to introduce a buck into a herd of does, or to hang a buck rag in the barn. A buck rag is an empty burlap sack or an old blanket that has been liberally rubbed over a mature buck's musk glands. Buck odor generally causes does to come into heat within about a week.

The fourth method is through light manipulation. Simulating the light conditions of fall prepares bucks and does for out-of-season breeding. An old method is to keep does indoors after the first of June and leave the lights on for only seven hours a day until they come into heat.

A more effective, but more complicated method has been devised at the International Dairy Goat Research Center at Texas A & M. It involves light-treating does for twenty hours a day over a sixty-day period, starting in early January, using one four-foot, forty-watt fluorescent tube for each forty-two square feet of floor space, hung at a height of eight to nine feet. The does are then kept under natural light for another thirty-five days. Into each pen of six does, a buck is introduced that has also been light-treated to stimulate fertility. He's left there for sixty days, during which two or three light-induced heat cycles occur. By this method, researchers achieved a pregnancy rate among Alpines of 67 percent, and 100 percent among Nubians.

Just how effectively you can control the occurrence of heat with buck scent or lighting depends on the season, the weather, your latitude, your management practices, and the age and breed of your does. Environmental control of estrus is easier with Nubians and Pygmies than with the Swiss breeds, for which hormonal treatment may be necessary for optimum results.

RECOGNIZING HEAT

A doe in heat will try to get as close as she can to a buck housed nearby. She'll moon around the nearest fence like a lovesick teenager, or run back and forth bleating and wagging her tail. If you take her to the buck, he'll paw and nibble at her, waggle his tongue, and issue gutteral grunts. He'll hang his muzzle in her falling urine, rub his beard in it when it puddles on the ground, and otherwise make a perfect fool of himself. The little lady will wag her tail, bleat, urinate, and squat. If you aren't there for the action, you may later detect what's happened by the ruffled or rubbed-off hair on the doe's tailhead, and the fresh abrasions around her vulva, the external opening to her genitals.

Other signs of heat to watch for are loss of appetite, frequent and insistent bleating, frequent urination, red or swollen vulva, drop in milk production, or a sudden increase about eight hours before heat symptoms appear.

Strings of mucus around her tail may also be a tip-off. At the beginning of heat, the mucus will be clear, but it will turn cloudy toward the time of ovulation. After the doe ovulates near the end of heat, the mucus will get thick and whitish. In addition to all this, some does do decidedly buckish things like ride other does, allow themselves to be ridden, or rub against other members of the herd. When such does become a nuisance, they need to be privately stalled until they calm down, which will happen either when they're bred or when heat ends.

If your does follow these textbook descriptions, consider yourself lucky. Many don't. Some just act a little strange. They may become nervous or be pushier than usual. It helps to learn the individual personalities and patterns of each of your does, and to jot down any changes. If you check for signs of heat daily during breeding season, and you know what is normal for each of your does, you can more easily detect changes as slight as being allowed to lift the tail of a doe that would otherwise be annoyed.

ABNORMAL HEAT		
Condition	**Cause**	**Treatment**
Weak or silent heat	Anemia	Treat for blood-sucking worms two weeks before breeding. Blood-test and treat for nutritional deficiencies.
Longer than normal cycles	Anemia;	Same as above.
	Embryonic death	Treatment is probably unnecessary since either embryonic materials become reabsorbed or abortion occurs.
Continuous heat; shorter than normal cycles	Cystic ovaries	Treat with hormones, which may not be successful if doe starts acting like a buck. When a regular heat period can be detected, successful breeding may be possible.
	Moldy feed; estrogen in some legume forages	Eliminate source.
Heat signs during pregnancy	Fairly common	No treatment necessary as ovulation does not occur.

A miniature version of the buck rag may help you detect heat. Rub a piece of cloth over the scent glands of a mature buck and keep it in a jar with a tight fitting lid to retain the odor. During your daily estrus check, open the jar and let each doe sniff the contents. If one is in heat, the signs should become more obvious.

One of the best heat-detectors is a buck wearing a breeding apron to prevent mating, or one that has been vasectomized. Pygmy bucks are terrific for this purpose because they eat less, making them more economical than larger bucks, and the little fellows perform the job with wholehearted enthusiasm.

Chapter 7

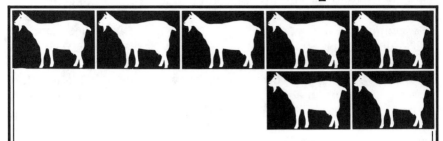

BREEDING
AND KIDDING

Controversy rages over when to breed a doe for the first time. Some herders advocate breeding as soon as a doe is able, perhaps not realizing that it may be as early as two months of age! A doe that is bred before she matures fully may become stunted since she cannot put nutrients into both her growth and fetal development. On the other hand, reasonably early breeding helps the udder mature, and a doe that's kept too long before being bred may never conceive, or if she does she may not be a good bearer or a good milker.

A well-nourished doe is ready for breeding earlier than a poorly fed one. It is therefore best to breed not by age but by weight. A doe should reach 65 to 75 percent of her mature weight before being bred. A properly fed doe will be ready at eight to nine months of age.

Prepare a doe for breeding by *flushing*—increasing her nutritional supply of energy to stimulate ovulation and conception. The idea is to have her put on weight for two or three weeks prior to breeding, and continue gaining until about three weeks afterwards. High quality forage may be used for flushing, or you can increase the concentrate ration. Thin does require a longer flushing period than ones in better condition.

A buck may be ready to breed at three or four months, depending on his breed, but it's best to use him only sparingly until he's at least six months old. The optimum frequency to use a buck for stud, whether for natural breeding or the collection of semen for artificial insemination, has not been fully studied. As a general rule, two or three times a week from the age of six months to one year are plenty. At maturity, a buck can handle twenty matings a week.

WHEN TO BREED

When does run together with a buck, they may kid more often than once a year. But dairy does are usually kept separate from bucks to prevent male odor from ruining the milk, and are bred annually to maximize milk flow. Does bred early in the season have better lactation records, and their female kids mature early enough to be bred the following season. But it's not necessarily desirable to breed a doe during her first heat of the season. You may wish to wait until her second or third heat to avoid having kids come during the worst part of winter, or to stagger freshening of your does to create a continuous milk flow.

The best time to breed a doe is in the middle of heat, but it's not always easy to tell when that occurs. You will be fairly safe to take the doe to the buck as soon as you notice she's in heat. If feasible, breed her again in about twelve hours to ensure conception. Rather than just leave a doe with the buck for a period of time, it's better to hand breed, which involves holding her by her collar or a lead. The buck will cooperate so quickly you'll wonder what all the fuss was about, and the doe will promptly calm down and be ready to return home.

If the buck shows little or no interest in your doe, you may have misjudged the signs of heat, or recognized them too late. Virgin does in particular are often hard to settle. Some keepers leave problem does with a stud for a full month, since bucks have an uncanny sense for right timing. But that's not always possible. The alternative is to keep an eye on your doe and on the calendar, and try again next time around.

If you don't own a buck, pick out a stud in advance and make arrangements early so you don't get caught in the breeding season rush. Look for a buck that is handsome and has a history of producing daughters with good milking records. Be sure to get a Service Memorandum signed by the buck's owner. It identifies the buck and doe, gives the date they were mated, and is required for registration of the offspring.

ARTIFICIAL INSEMINATION

Natural breeding is still more popular than artificial insemination (A.I.) because breeding by buck is both easier and surer. In most cases A.I. costs about the same as stud service, and both can be less expensive than keeping a stud for only a small herd. A.I. is especially important where good stud bucks are not available locally. A.I. lets you take advantage of a wide range of superior bucks from across the country. And you can keep a closed herd to prevent the spread of diseases, since A.I. sires are screened for health problems transmitted through sexual contact.

Some vets perform artificial insemination. More and more goatkeepers are learning how, and many are willing to do it for others. The initial investment is fairly high, but can be mitigated if a group of compatible herders or members of a club pool resources. The semen storage tank is the most costly piece of equipment. It is used to keep the semen at

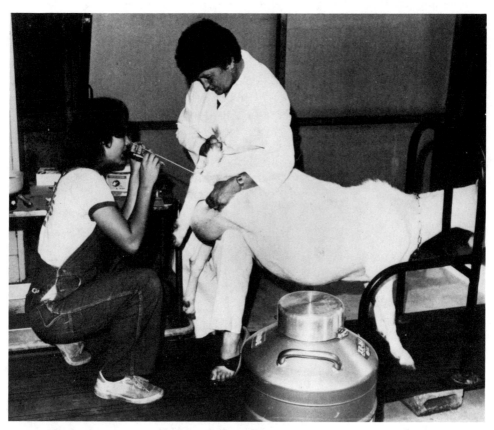

Artificial insemination must be timed carefully with ovulation.
(Photo courtesy of the Dairy Goat Research Facility,
University of California, Davis, California)

a temperature of $-320°F$ during transportation and storage. After semen is selected according to the histories of stud bucks published in various catalogs, it is delivered by bus in the processor's transporting tank. The breeder must have another tank for the semen, so the processor's tank can be promptly returned.

Several schools scattered across the country teach A.I. through intensive crash courses, usually one day long. Performing A.I. requires good detection of estrus. Since sperm is viable only eight to twelve hours after being thawed—in contrast to as much as two and a half days for natural semen—it is critical that insemination be well coordinated with ovulation. Some herders keep a buck to stimulate ovulation and help them identify does in heat, even though they use A.I. to breed their does to superior distant studs.

Conception rates very between 50 and 70 percent. Some practitioners are more successful than others because they are more sensitive, often through longer experience, to the many factors involved. Rough handling of does during the procedure, for instance, reduces the chances of conception and increases the possibility of early embryonic death.

It helps ensure success if you talk gently to your doe to reassure her throughout the procedure. Unless you do your own A.I., you may have to transport the doe, which increases stress if she's not used to traveling. If you have a large herd in which estrus synchronization is feasible, you may be able to talk the practitioner into coming to your place to do a group.

Whether you do your own A.I. or hire someone else, be sure to have documentation similar to a Service Memorandum for natural service. A Record of Artificial Insemination should include the date and identify the doe, buck, semen processor, and inseminator.

FAILURE TO CONCEIVE

Failure to conceive is less often the fault of the buck or doe than of the inexperienced herder whose timing was off. Breeding a doe only a few hours late may cause failure.

A bacterial or viral infection of the vagina may also prevent settling. Affected does come into heat but do not conceive because the change in vaginal pH kills sperm. The condition usually corrects itself in time. It may be treated with a douche after a veterinary diagnosis determines the cause of infection. Meanwhile, A.I. may be used to bypass the vagina and put the sperm right into the uterus.

If a doe gives birth and then fails to come back into heat the following season, she could have a *retained corpus luteum*, a fairly common problem in dairy goats. When an egg is released from the ovary, a temporary yellowish mass of glandular tissue develops at the spot from which the egg was released. This yellow body, the corpus luteum, releases progesterone, which causes estrus to subside, seals off the womb, and otherwise aids pregnancy. At the time the doe is ready to kid, her body produces the female hormone estrogen, which causes the corpus luteum to become reabsorbed. If there is a hormonal malfunction, the corpus luteum will fail to regress, and will continue producing progesterone so that the doe cannot come back into heat. An injection or two of estrogen usually corrects the problem.

Conception failure may not be the doe's fault, but the buck's. Overbreeding desirable studs is a common cause. Fat bucks that don't get enough exercise may suffer reduced fertility. Hormonal imbalance and nutritional deficiencies are also possibilities. Undescended testicles (*cryptorchidism*) play havoc with fertility, and can occur in bucks of any breed. In rare cases where both testicles are retained, the buck produces no semen. Usually, though, only one fails to descend, or descends late, and that testicle will be sterile. The condition is usually hereditary, so a buck should not be bred even if his testicle eventually descends and he appears normal.

Intersex

One of the most important causes of infertility in dairy goats, both bucks and does, is lack of proper development of the reproductive organs in a condition called *hermaphroditism, genital hypoplasia,* or *intersex*. It can appear in any breed, most often in offspring of two naturally hornless goats. It may also occur when one parent is horned and the other polled. The gene for hornlessness somehow inhibits normal development of the reproductive organs. Affected goats may have abnormal external genitals, but many are not so easy to identify. If you have suspicions about a particular animal, have a goat-oriented vet make a thorough examination to save you time and heartache. As soon as you identify them, do away with intersexual animals since they are useless for breeding, and even their meat tastes strong and bucky.

ABORTION

If you thought your doe was pregnant, but she comes back into heat, she may have aborted. Goats are probably more susceptible to abortion than any other livestock. Among the causes are disease, poor nutrition, poisoning, interference with or absence of a corpus luteum, or an abnormal fetus that is naturally rejected by the doe.

Injury is a common cause. Does often get into butting sessions with each other, especially if one is a newcomer to the herd. A pregnant doe should not roughhouse with other goats, nor climb and jump. If one tends to be overly active, move her to a private stall where she will enjoy a more sedate pregnancy. Avoid procedures such as hoof trimming that might cause her to struggle. Vaccinate against abortion-causing diseases endemic in your area, such as leptospirosis and vibriosis.

When a doe aborts, it's important to determine whether it was due to some condition of stress or whether the doe is a habitual aborter. If the fetus is aborted live, or freshly dead, suspect stress. Look for ways to improve your management. Don't be overly concerned with the occasional abortion.

If the aborted fetus is dead and swelling, or already decomposing, the doe is probably a habitual aborter and should be culled. If you experience herd-wide abortion problems, or characteristic premature kidding in first fresheners, discuss with your vet the need for treatment against infectious agents such as chlamydia.

Detecting abortion isn't always easy, especially during the first three months of pregnancy when the fetus remains fairly small and when it is not uncommon for a doe to appear to come back into heat. Signs are bloody discharge and behavioral changes including loss of appetite, dazed condition, and hanging back from the others. If you suspect abortion, watch for the expulsion of the placenta, and consult a vet about the need to take precautionary health measures. Don't rebreed an aborted doe until the following season.

GESTATION

In the likeliest case, your doe will experience a normal pregnancy. For the first three months, you'll see little change, and it will be nearly impossible to tell whether she's pregnant. Tests can tell you for sure. Testing is done through a vet, diagnostic laboratory, or mail-in service. The most feasible for small herds is to check milk or urine for *estrone sulfate*, a hormone produced by a living fetus that can be detected as early as thirty-five days after conception. If it turns out the doe is not pregnant, you may still have time to rebreed her. When it's too late for rebreeding, you may milk her right through to the next breeding season, though she won't give as much as she would if freshened. A doe that has been successfully bred should be dried off three months later so that milk production won't compete with fetal development.

Unborn kids put on 70 percent of their weight during the last six weeks of gestation. About a month before kidding, your doe should really fill out. Start feeding her a little grain on the milk stand both to readjust her to the milking routine and to check her udder and watch for possible problems. Two or three weeks before kidding, restrict legume roughage and calcium supplements in the rations of high producers.

Exactly when your doe will kid depends on several factors. Older and poorly fed does tend to kid late. Multiple births usually shorten the gestation period. During the last week or two before kidding, the doe may develop depressed areas on both sides of her tail, and hollowness at her hips. She may carry the kids lower so that her pelvic bones seem sharper, and her pinbones become raised. Her vulva may distend. Her udder may fill out. If the udder of a heavy milker becomes tight and shiny, milk her out to prevent damage to the ligaments supporting the udder. Close to five months after she was bred, your doe may become withdrawn, bleat, eat less, and discharge white mucus. Her time is near.

Although the gestation period is 150 days, a doe fills out most during the last six weeks. (Photo by Matto)

FACTORS INFLUENCING
HEAT, FERTILITY, AND CONCEPTION

Abortion   Injury; disease; poor nutrition; poisoning; improperly working corpus luteum.

Artificial insemination   Improper semen handling; bad timing; poor technique.

False pregnancy   Cause is unknown; future pregnancies likely to be normal.

Condition   Overly fat buck or doe; disease.

Flushing   Promotes easier heat detection; chance for multiple births.

Intersex   Occurs most often in offspring of two polled goats; has no cure.

Light   Decreasing photoperiod, either natural or artificial; subject buck and does to same light condition.

Overbreeding studs   Young bucks should be bred no more than two or three times a week, mature bucks not over twenty times a week.

FACTORS INFLUENCING
HEAT, FERTILITY, AND CONCEPTION (Con't.)

Nutrition	Deficiencies.
Owner inexperience	Failure to identify heat; poor timing in coordinating breeding with ovulation.
Reproductive disorders	Retained corpus luteum; infertile sperm; abnormal egg; hormonal malfunction.
Season	Swiss breeds come into heat from end of September to end of January; Nubians and Pygmies from mid-September to early January and maybe other times.
Social	Presence or odor of active buck.
Stress	Transporting; weather conditions; rough handling, especially during A.I.
Temperature	Buck fertility is low above 85°F. Conception is also reduced by warm weather.
Vaginal infection	Bacterial or viral infection may cause sperm death after mating.

REPRODUCTION RECAP

Breeding season	Early fall to mid-winter; longer for Pygmies and Nubians.

DOES

Puberty	4 to 8 months; should weigh 80 lbs. at first breeding.
Heat cycle	17 to 23 days; 19 is average.
Heat duration	
natural	12 to 36 hours; 18 is average.
light-induced	8 to 10 hours.
Gestation	147 to 156 days; 150 is average.
Number of kids	1 to 3; 2 is average; 4–6 possible.

BUCKS

Puberty	3 to 4 months; should be 6 months old for regular breeding.
Breeding frequency	2 to 3 times a week to age one year; up to 20 times a week thereafter.
Sperm viability	
natural	24 to 36 hours.
frozen and thawed	8 to 12 hours.

KIDDING

Some goats wander off quietly and kid by themselves. Others, especially ones that thrive on human contact, will let you know when they're ready so you'll be there for moral support. It's a good idea to be on hand in the unlikely event the doe needs your help, but don't be embarrassed if you miss it all because you didn't realize what was happening. Even experienced herders have been surprised suddenly to find newborn kids scampering about.

Have a roomy stall prepared where the bedding is fresh and clean for the health of the newborn. Take the doe there when she seems ready. She may paw the ground, lie down and get up restlessly, pant, or rearrange the bedding. Or she may lie down and not get up until her first kid is born. She may labor for several hours before she actually kids. When contractions get closer together at the start of hard labor, she'll pass gelatinous strings of bloody mucus. The first kid should be no more than fifteen minutes away, and the entire process should take about forty-five minutes, depending on the number of kids being born.

There will likely be two, though three or four are not uncommon, especially in Pygmies and Nubians. A single is possible for a doe's first kidding.

When birthing starts, you'll see a round, dark, bulging water bag. It will burst to reveal two feet with a tiny nose resting on them. Soon out come shoulders, hips, and back legs. Delight in the spectacle, but don't interfere or you'll upset the doe and may cause unnecessary complications.

Sometimes kids come out back legs first. After the water bag ruptures, you'll see two feet with the toes pointing upward instead of downward, and no visible head. This position is easier on the doe because the bulging head and shoulders of the kid do not come through so abruptly. But sometimes the umbilical cord breaks before the kid gets its head out of the birth canal. The kid will begin to breath and may suffocate from inhaled fluids. Make sure that doesn't happen by lending a gentle helping hand. When you see the shoulders, take hold of the kid and press firmly downward as the doe pushes. Never pull or jerk the kid out.

The afterbirth, or *placenta*, usually comes out at the time of kidding or just afterwards. It's a stringy, light, thin, milky-looking membrane. In a multiple birth, there may be one or more. The doe may consume the placenta as a natural source of protein, and if she does she'll not be very hungry for the next few days. If eating of the placenta offends you, or if the doe declines to consume it, remove and burn or bury it.

In most cases, that's all there is to the business of kidding.

POST-KIDDING DOE CARE

If your doe seems perfectly comfortable half an hour after giving birth, she's probably had all the kids she's going to. Offer her a drink of warm water both to replace lost fluids and to relax her and encourage the release of any remaining afterbirth. For a special treat, and to replace lost energy, add a little honey or molasses to the warm water. The doe will probably not be ready to eat until her next regular feeding, but just in case be sure she has fresh hay, and offer half her usual grain ration or some warm bran mash. If you really want to spoil her, give her a little warm oatmeal or a handful of raisins.

The top of her bedding will be wet and slimy. Remove it with as little fuss as possible since the doe will be tired and want to rest. She may continue a little bloody discharge for the next two weeks, which is normal. Help her stay clean by clipping the hair around her tail and udder. If she has kidded during warm weather, she may shed quite a bit. Keep her neat with a good daily brushing. Over the next two weeks, gradually increase her grain ration until she's back on her regular milk-production feeding program.

ABNORMAL KIDDING

If your doe is in hard labor for half an hour and nothing seems to be happening, it's possible she's just taking her time. On the other hand, something could be going wrong that requires you to play James Herriot. A kid may be trying to come out wrong way around, or several kids may have gotten tangled together while trying to decide who should go first.

Trim your nails. Scrub your hands and arms with a mild dish soap, and wash and dry the doe's vulva. Lubricate your hands and arms with the same dish soap or with Vaseline or KY Jelly.

Reach in, try to figure out what's happening, and rearrange things to get one kid into either of the two normal positions. Whenever you move a hoof into the birth canal, cup your hand over it to avoid tearing the doe's uterus, which could lead to infection or cause her to bleed to death. Always be certain you know what you're holding, and that all the parts you rearrange belong to the same kid. Afterwards, as a precaution against uterine infection, administer antibiotic injections or a vaginal bolus obtained from your vet, or have the vet check the doe over and treat her.

It's important to know when to play the hero and when to call in a veterinarian. If your doe has been in hard labor for more than forty-five minutes and you've been helping for fifteen minutes without success, pick up the phone. Don't wait much longer or she'll be all tuckered out and harder to help. If you can't find a goat-oriented vet, try for an experienced goatkeeper or even a neighboring sheepherder. As a last resort, you won't be the first frantic goat owner to prevail on your family doctor.

Chapter 8

KID CARE

As soon as a kid is born, the doe will lick it to stimulate blood flow and to clean it off. You can help by clearing the kid's nose and mouth with a clean towel so it won't breath in fluids or suffocate. If the kid doesn't start breathing right away, or isn't breathing well, hold it upside down by its hind legs so fluids can drain out. Give it a smack on the side with your open hand to cause it to inhale and begin normal breathing.

If the umbilical cord is still attached, tie it off about two inches from the kid's navel with a soft cord and cut it with sharp, clean scissors. The remaining piece will dry up and fall off in about three weeks. Pour a little iodine in a small jar, hold the jar against the kid's belly with the navel inside the jar, and slosh the iodine to coat the area around the navel. If the temperature in the goat barn is below freezing, supply heat up to 40°F. As soon as possible, preferably within fifteen minutes of birth, see that the kid gets its first feeding of colostrum.

Feeding kids heat-treated colostrum and milk is an important health care measure. (Photo courtesy of Future Farms of America, Alexandria, Virginia)

COLOSTRUM

A kid is born without natural protection from disease. It acquires immunity from its mother through her first milk—*colostrum*—a thick, yellow substance that not only contains antibodies against disease in the mother's environment, but also acts as a laxative to remove digestive residue and prevent hard droppings that might irritate the kid's intestine. If you raise your kids naturally, encourage them to nuzzle and nurse as soon as possible. Otherwise, milk out some of the colostrum and hand feed it to them.

Most does produce colostrum from around the time of freshening to up to four days afterward. It should be the exclusive food of kids for their first two days of life. Extra may be fed back to the doe to restore important minerals and vitamins to her system, or may be refrigerated or frozen for later use. Heavy milkers that do not dry off completely prior to kidding may not produce colostrum, so it pays to have some in the freezer. Warm it to body temperature before feeding.

Researchers at Washington State University have found that heat-treating all colostrum and milk before feeding it to kids reduces the spread of certain diseases and leads to healthier herds. This requires hand-feeding kids right from the start. If you can't be absolutely certain you'll be there for the kidding, the mother's teats must be sealed with tape (purchased through dairy goat suppliers) to prevent nursing. One accidental feeding from the teat can undo all your good work.

Harmful organisms in colostrum are destroyed by heating it to 130°F and holding it at that temperature for one hour. Use a double boiler or a crock pot to prevent scorching, or heat the colostrum to 135°F and pour it into a heated thermos that will keep it sufficiently warm for an hour. Cool the colostrum to body temperature before feeding. Do not heat it above 140°F or the useful antibodies will be destroyed. Give each kid half a cup per feeding, up to one pound maximum each day, in at least two feedings but preferably four or five evenly spaced ones.

FEEDING

A kid is born essentially as a simple-stomached animal since the first three chambers of its digestive system are undeveloped and only the fourth is active. Until its rumen becomes active, a kid can digest only milk. In nature it would nurse, but nursing is hard on the udder of a doe kept as a dairy animal, and you can't heat-treat milk for disease control. In addition, a nursing doe sniffs and snorts at every moving thing so that her kids grow up skittish and suspicious. For these reasons, many herders hand feed their kids.

KID FEEDING SCHEDULE

Age	Feed	Amount	Number of feedings
1–2 days	colostrum (100°F)	1# max*	½ C per feeding, 4–5 times a day at evenly spaced intervals
3–7 days	milk or milk replacer	2# max*	1 C per feeding, 3–4 times a day, evenly spaced
2–6 weeks	milk or milk replacer	2#*	2 C per feeding, twice a day
	water	–	free choice
	grain	introduce	each feeding
	hay	–	free choice
6–8 weeks	milk or milk replacer	1.5#**	evenly divided in two feedings
	water	–	free choice
	grain	0.5#***	evenly divided in two feedings
	hay	–	free choice
2 months to 1 year	milk or milk replacer	none	(wean)
	water	–	free choice
	grain	1#***	evenly divided in two feedings
	hay	–	free choice

*Daily total of whole milk or milk replacer should be no less than 15 percent of kid's body weight, and no more than 25 percent. Pygmy kids need about half the listed quantities. Keeping kids on the hungry side encourages early eating of solid foods.

**Around sixth week, gradually begin reducing milk so that none is fed by the eighth week when kid is weaned.

***Exact amount of grain depends on kid's size and growth rate. Cut back if you can't feel the ribs of a kid in the large breeds, or if you can grab a handful of flesh from behind a Pygmy elbow. If hay is of lesser quality, more grains will be needed for nutritional balance and proper growth.

A variety of bottles, nipples, and pans is available for hand feeding. One of the cheapest is a nipple that fits over a standard pop bottle. To train kids to drink from the nipple, dip it in milk and let the kid have a taste. The rest will come naturally.

Feeding kids from a shallow pan is easy, requires no special equipment, and has the advantage that kids learn to lap right from the beginning, simplifying weaning. To teach a kid to drink from a pan, gently dip its mouth into milk until it has a taste and starts to drink. This may require patient repetition. Always wash and sanitize nipples, bottles, and pans after each feeding to avoid undesirable bacteria that make kids very sick.

If you begin with heat-treated colostrum, continue heat-treating the milk by pasteurizing it. Heat it to 145°F and hold it there for half an hour, or heat it to 165°F for thirty seconds, stirring occasionally to prevent scorching. A home pasteurizing unit will simplify things and save you time. Cool the milk to body temperature before feeding.

If you can't be home for frequent feeding, you can provide free choice milk in a pail designed with a chamber for ice to prevent spoilage. Cold milk does not seem to affect kids if they get used to it gradually. Alternatively, use the old-time method of inoculating milk with *Strep. cremoris* buttermilk culture to keep it from spoiling at room temperature. Half a cup of commercial buttermilk will do the trick, carrying some over to inoculate the next batch.

Milk Replacer

If you need your does' milk, or if you don't have enough to go around, you can use cow milk, powdered whole milk, or milk replacer. Kids fed goat milk for at least three weeks have no problem handling milk replacers. Try to find a formula designed specifically for kids, such as the one by Land O' Lakes. Calf replacer is lower in protein. Lamb replacer is higher in fat, but, of the two, is better for kids. Use replacers with milk solids and not vegetable protein. Start out by mixing the substitute with goat milk, gradually reducing the amount of milk and increasing the amount of replacer. If you plan to sell kids, switching them over to replacer makes it easier for the new owner to continue the same feeding program.

Weaning

When the kids are two weeks old, offer hay free choice, even if they have access to fresh pasture, since kids need dry hay for rumen development. Also introduce a little grain. If you're pan feeding, sprinkle some grain in the milk or water to encourage the kids to eat. It's important to get them eating solid foods, so offer a variety of tantalizing tidbits such as comfrey leaves, sunflower seeds, and vegetable trimmings.

When kids start eating well, be sure they have access to fresh water. Wean by about eight weeks, or when kids triple their birth weight and are chewing their cuds. As weaning time approaches, gradually substitute water for some of their milk until they're drinking entirely water. They'll be weaned without even noticing.

The next few months in a kid's life are critical. If you feed a balanced ration for good growth, doelings will develop the capacity for maximum milk production and be ready to breed early.

A COMPLETE 16% STARTER RATION

Feed	%
Corn	27.6%
Crimped oats	37.9%
Soybean meal (44%)	10.0%
Alfalfa leaf meal	18.0%
Cane molasses	5.0%
Trace mineral salt	1.0%
Limestone	.3%
Vitamin A, D, E premix	.2%

From: Thian H. Teh, et al, "Raising Goat Kids—the Artificial Way." International Dairy Goat Research Center Bulletin, Volume A1, No. 1, March 1985.

TATTOOING

All kids should be tattooed as soon after birth as possible for positive identification. For most breeds the tattoo goes in the ear. LaManchas are tattooed in the tail web. Generally a tattoo will include herd identification letters assigned by a registry, along with a code for the year, and a number signifying the order of entry into your herd for that year, whether by birth or by purchase. Each animal in your herd will thus have a different tattoo. Tattooing instruments with directions are sold by many livestock suppliers.

TATTOO YEAR CODE			
T	= 1983	A = 1989
V	= 1984	B = 1990
W	= 1985	C = 1991
X	= 1986	D = 1992
Y	= 1987	E = 1993
Z	= 1988	F = 1994

To avoid confusion, G, I, O, Q, and U are never used.

Note: The Canadian registry uses a different system.

CLIPPING WATTLES

Wattles are optional appendages that may appear in any breed. They're long, thin bags of skin hanging below the neck. Usually there are two, but sometimes there's only one. No function has ever been found for them, but goats with the genetic trait for wattles seem to be more prolific than those without.

Wattles can be a nusiance. One goat may suck or chew on those of another, and they get torn when hung up in brush or fences. Removing them gives a cleaner neckline to dairy animals. Wattles may be snipped off young goats with clean, sharp scissors. The minor wound heals without a scar.

Removing hornbuds when kids are still young is a lot less painful than waiting until their horns begin to grow. Naturally hornless kids don't require disbudding, and can be identified by the looser skin on the top of their heads, and the straighter hair over their horn spots. If the skin is tight and there is curly hair over the hornbuds, you must disbud.

There are several ways to do it, but the best is to use an electric disbudder with a three-quarter- to one-inch tip, purchased through a livestock supplier. The kid will holler bloody murder, so your first time around you may want to have an experienced person there to reassure you that you aren't killing the poor creature.

Kids should be between one and two weeks of age, in good health, and growing well when this is done. Heat the disbudder red hot and

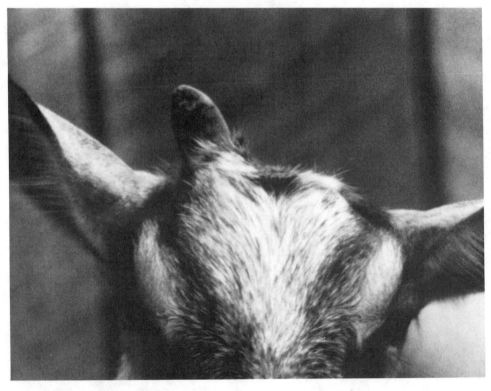

If disbudding is improper, a repeat of the procedure is required to avoid scurs such as this one. (Photo by Matto)

apply it for ten seconds, rotating slightly without rubbing. There should be two copper-colored rings when you're through. Treat them with antiseptic ointment. The hornbuds should fall off in about six weeks. Watch for any sign of horn growth, indicating an imperfect job, and disbud again if necessary to prevent scurs.

Some herders charge a nominal fee to disbud for those who don't care to do it themselves, or don't raise enough goats to invest in the equipment. Some goat clubs sponsor disbudding workshops, and many 4-H groups organize local demonstrations.

DE-SCENTING

At the time of disbudding, you may also want to remove the scent glands on the heads of uncastrated buck kids. The glands are located behind the hornbuds and slightly closer together. They can be burned out with the electric disbudding iron or you can have them surgically removed as described in chapter 4. Castrated bucks do not develop buck odor and therefore do not require de-scenting.

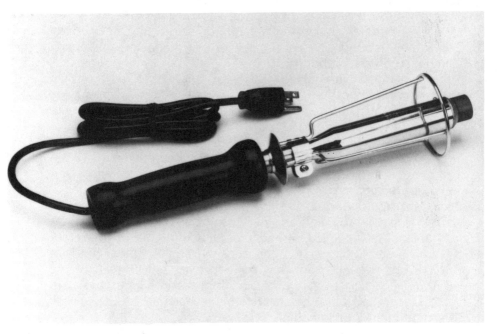

This iron is used for disbudding and to de-scent uncastrated bucklings.
(Photo courtesy of NASCO, Fort Atkinson, Wisconsin)

CASTRATING

Surplus bucklings should be castrated as soon as their testicles descend into the scrotum, between the age of seven days and three weeks. Once they're castrated, they are called *wethers*, and are raised for meat, used for draft, or sold as pets.

Of the various castrating methods, probably the easiest for most goatkeepers is to use an *elastrator*, a device that stretches a rubber ring so it can be placed around the base of the scrotum. The nine-inch elastrator sold for lambs is the right size for kids. When the ring is released, it cuts off circulation. Within a few weeks the scrotum atrophies and falls off, leaving a smooth belly. Other castrating methods leave a hanging empty sack.

Although use of an elastrator is bloodless, bucklings should be vaccinated for tetanus prior to castration. When directions are carefully followed, discomfort lasts only about an hour. As with disbudding, if you castrate few bucklings a year, you can probably find a fellow goatkeeper who will do it for you for a nominal fee, saving the cost of purchasing equipment.

GENERAL CARE

Kids of approximately the same age may be kept together in a stall in the goat shelter, or in their own private housing. Many herders use light portable hutches or ones constructed on skids that can be easily moved to new ground after each batch of kids graduates, preventing a build-up of disease pathogens.

Change bedding often, since kids keep it pretty wet. Let them get plenty of sunshine, fresh air, and daily exercise. A play platform will keep them fit, and you'll have fun watching them enjoy their favorite game, King of the Mountain.

Keep a record sheet on each kid. The first entries should be weight at birth, heart girth, and height at the withers. Keep a record of the growth of each kid by weighing them every two weeks, to help determine if your feeding program is adequate, and to warn of any health problems that may be inhibiting growth.

Check kids early for birth anomalies and defects. The sooner you identify animals to be culled, the easier it will be to control your emotional attachment. Look for such things as overshot or undershot jaw, deformities, intersexuality, and any traits that are not correct for the breed. Watch for extra teats in both bucklings and doelings. These can be removed surgically, but the characteristic is hereditary so it's unwise to use such animals for breeding.

Handling and Training

When you handle a kid to check it over, or perform any procedure, sit down and put it on your lap or between your knees. For disbudding, it's convenient to tie the kid in a burlap sack with a small hole in one corner for the head. If you reinforce the head hole, or tighten it with a drawstring, the kid will not be able to poke its front legs out. You can also restrain a kid in a stout cardboard box with a hole cut in one corner for the head. The box should be just big enough for the animal to fit into, but not so roomy that it can draw in its head and squirm around—24" long by 16" high by 5" deep is about right for young kids. Secure the box shut with strong twine. Containers called disbudding boxes are used to hold kids for disbudding, de-scenting, and, if modified with an opening at the back, for giving shots. A restraining container makes it easier when you work on kids singlehanded.

Start training kids early. Put a collar around the neck of each and use it to direct the kid whenever you handle it. Work with kids at least ten minutes a day, which may include feeding time, to assure tameness and easier handling later on. Talk to each, using its name often until it learns to come when you call. Do not let kids out of their yard to play or you'll encourage their desire to escape.

Kids like these LaManchas enjoy climbing on a play platform, and it helps them to grow strong. (Photo by Matto)

KID HEALTH

The main health problems to watch for in kids are diarrhea and constipation. A kid's first bowel movement is thick and dark, and occurs within a few hours after birth. Subsequent bowel movements are yellowish and clumpy, changing, as the kid grows, to small pellets similar to those expelled by adult goats. Any other change may indicate health problems.

Diarrhea in kids is often caused by eating too much or too fast. Reduce the amount you feed at one time, and feed more often. If that doesn't help, substitute water for half the milk ration for forty-eight hours.

Severe diarrhea, called *scours*, requires elimination of milk. Treatment with keopectate may be necessary to prevent dehydration. If you pinch a kid's skin and it sticks together, you need to use an electrolyte to replace lost body fluids—fast! Scours may result from nutritional problems, but may also indicate infection, most often caused by *E. coli*. If you can't clear up the diarrhea right away, have a sample cultured by a vet to determine if medical treatment is necessary.

Constipation may result from overfeeding, too coarse rations, lack of exercise, or lack of water. A kid may have difficulty passing feces, strain, and expel hard, dry pellets. Ensuring a pure water supply and plenty of exercise helps, and so does a laxative feedstuff such as bran. Serious cases may require a warm, soapy enema.

If you keep your kids in a clean environment from birth, feed them properly, see that they get plenty of exercise and sunshine, and vaccinate according to the requirements of your area, they'll grow fast and strong with a minimum of health problems.

ELECTROLYTE FORMULA

Solution	Dose
White Karo syrup or honey	2 tablespoons
Table salt	½ teaspoon
Baking soda	¼ teaspoon
Water, purified	to 1 quart

Use as soon as diarrhea is noticed. Make sure solution is mixed thoroughly. Make up a fresh batch daily to feed in place of milk at double the usual rate. Use for one and a half to two days, then return to regular milk diet.

DISEASES OF KIDS

Disease	Symptom	Prevention
Coccidiosis	Temporary loss of appetite; soft, bloody feces	Avoid overcrowding and poor sanitation.
Colibacillosis; E. coli Septicemia; Diarrhea; Scours	Diarrhea; dehydration; coma; death	Strict sanitation where kids are born and raised; feed colostrum soon after birth; prevent excessive eating; avoid inferior milk replacers.
Hypoglycemia; Birth chilling	Shivering; arched back; hair standing on end; stiffness; coma; death	Early feeding of colostrum.
Navel ill; Omphalitis; Arthritis	Abscessed belly button; depression; fever; hot, arthritic joints	Heat-treat colostum and milk; provide clean birthing stall; liberally apply iodine to umbilical cord at birth.
Pneumonia	Respiratory sounds	Heat-treat colostrum and milk; provide good ventilation; avoid overcrowding, overheating, dust, and condensation in housing.
Salmonellosis; Bloody Scours; Black Scours	High fever; smelly black or bloody diarrhea; passing clear mucus and shredded tissue	Avoid stress; cull carriers.

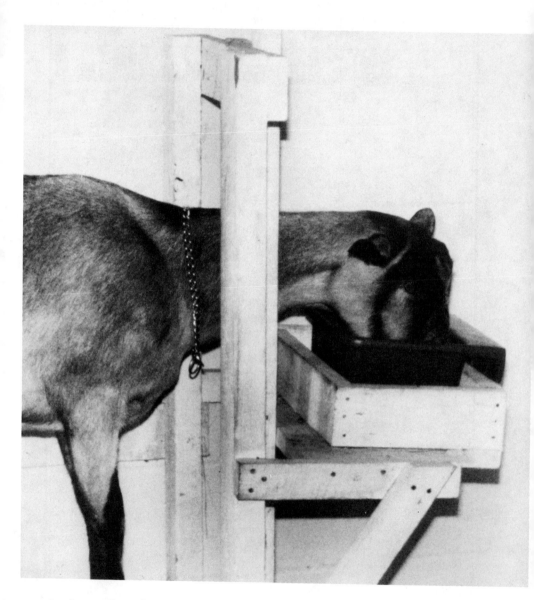

Feeding on the milk stand. (Photo by Matto)

Chapter 9

GOAT MILK

Milk—that's what raising dairy goats is all about. On a worldwide basis, more goat milk than cow milk is drunk. Goat milk contains many different types of protein, some of which are similar to those in cow milk, and may cause the same type of allergic reactions in people who cannot tolerate milk. But other proteins in goat milk differ from the ones in cow milk. So, depending on the cause of the allergy, a reaction to cow milk may not be triggered by goat milk. In addition, goat milk has smaller fat particles and softer curd, making it easier to digest. A properly managed goat produces milk that tastes almost exactly like cow milk, but it's whiter. The precise composition and flavor vary with the breed, the herd, specific herd management, and the individual doe.

In nature, a doe gives milk until her kids are weaned, and then she dries off. We're able to extend the lactation period to ten months or more through knowledgeable feeding and regular milking to stimulate continuous flow. Good production depends on age, breed, genetic ability, feeding, health care, and the doe's sense of security and well-being. A good doe in her prime should give at least a gallon from just after freshening to about five or six months later, then taper down to three quarts. By the eighth month she may give two quarts, and by the ninth or tenth month she may give only a quart. A Pygmy will give approximately one-third as much as a larger doe. In dairy practice, milk is not measured by volume but is weighed in pounds and tenths of a pound. Weighing is more accurate, especially when milk is fresh and has a head of foam. A pint of milk weighs approximately a pound, exact weight depending on the butterfat content.

Most people try to increase milk production, but if you're getting more milk than you need, you can reduce production by decreasing grain intake. Alternatively, consider sharing or selling excess milk, or using it to raise pigs or calves.

MILKING PROCEDURE

The initial milking procedure is the same whether you milk by hand or use a milking machine. Cleanliness is essential for good tasting milk. Any little bit of manure, dust, or hair that gets into the milk may change its flavor. Begin by brushing the doe to remove loose hair and dirt. Then, with warm water containing a dairy sanitizer, wash dirt from her udder and flank, with particular attention to the teats. Washing not only removes soil, but also stimulates the doe to get her ready for milking. Dry the teats and your hands with a soft paper towel, using a fresh one for each doe.

AVERAGE MILK SOLIDS

Type	Percentage of Total	What it Does for You
Fat	3.8%	Warmth
Protein	3.0%	Growth and muscles
Lactose	4.1%	Energy
Minerals	1.8%	General well-being
Total Solids	12.7%	

As you prepare the udder and teats for milking, check for anything unusual—wounds, developing lumps, excessive warmth or coolness—that may indicate trouble. At least once a week, aim the first few squirts of milk from each teat into a strip cup or strip plate designed to check for irregularities that indicate problems in the udder. This first milk may contain bacteria from the teat ends, and should be discarded anyway.

If you have a fairly large herd, you may wish to milk by machine. But it takes a lot of goats to justify the cost, and unless you can milk at least two goats at once, it's just as fast to milk by hand. A milking machine is a definite plus if you have any disability that makes hand milking difficult.

How To Milk

Most owners of small herds milk by hand. There is only one way to learn to milk, and that's by doing it. No amount of textbook description will substitute for the real thing. It's easier to learn on an experienced doe, since a first freshener may be skittish, and her teat openings will be tight, making things hard on the nervous, inexperienced milker.

Start by getting the doe stationary and getting yourself in a comfortable position so you can milk without straining your back and arms. Always milk from the same side—the choice is yours. If you acquire a doe that's been milked from the other side, it will take time and patience to retrain her.

Think of the udder as a big, milk-filled glove with the teats as fingers. There are tiny holes at the bottom of each finger, and you have to squeeze the fingers to squirt the milk out the holes. Unless you use your thumb and index finger to close off the opening into the palm of the glove, the milk will squeeze back upward instead of out the holes. Use the rest of your fingers to put firm pressure against the teat and move the flow of milk downward. As you empty each teat, release the pressure so more milk will flow in. Work slowly and rhythmically, squeezing out the milk without pulling down on the teats.

When the flow slows, gently bump and massage the udder to let more milk down. Then start milking again. When there is no more milk, the teats will become soft and pliable like the fingers of a quality kid glove. Don't try to strip out every last drop or you may damage the teats.

When you're done, use a commercial teat dip to seal off the teat ends and prevent infection, and rub the teats and lower part of the udder with a dairy ointment such as Bag Balm to keep them from getting chapped. Then let out the doe and prepare to milk the next one.

Handling the Does

Always milk in the same order, preferably starting with the herd queen and continuing according to the established pecking order of your does. Let only one goat into the milking area at a time, or others may interfere with the procedure. Keep the doe calm by talking to her while you work. She'll be less likely to get restless if she's busy eating her grain ration while you milk. If you take too long, or she isn't used to being milked, a doe may prance around, kick the milk pail, or stamp a foot square in it.

Pygmies are somewhat more difficult to break to milking than other breeds, perhaps because their smaller teats and udders require gentler handling. Control restless movements by leaning against the doe with your arm or shoulder. For a persistent kicker, tie a cord around the hocks of her rear legs and hold it down with your foot, or have someone hold her feet while you work. As she gets the idea, and you become more proficient, things will go a lot more smoothly.

Milk production ceases when the udder becomes full, so try to milk at regular intervals as close to twelve hours apart as possible. Heavy milkers will produce more if you milk them three times a day.

EQUIPMENT

Milk into a stainless steel seamless milk pail that's easy to clean and won't interact with elements in the milk. If the pail has a hood or partial cover, debris is less likely to fall in. You also need a strainer, disposable milk filters, and easy-to-clean jars for storing the milk.

All equipment for milking and milk storage must be kept strictly clean to avoid off-flavors and spoilage. After milking, rinse equipment in cool or lukewarm water before washing. Hot water causes milk protein to crust on the surface of equipment. Follow up with hot water and a detergent, using a stiff brush rather than a sponge or dish cloth. A regular dairy sanitizer keeps equipment sparkling clean. Once or twice a week, use a commercial dairy acid cleaner to prevent the buildup of mineral deposits.

Store milking equipment and utensils in a clean, dust-free place. Rinse cleaned equipment again before you milk and, to be on the safe side, clean it once more with a dairy sanitizer according to label directions. All this cleaning may seem like a lot of extra work, but your reward will be the best milk you've ever tasted.

MINIMUM MILKING EQUIPMENT

Equipment	Remarks
Seamless milk pail	Stainless steel, preferably with a hood or partial cover.
Strainer and milk filters	Filters are not reusable, so keep plenty on hand.
Storage containers	Easy-to-clean half-gallon canning jars are ideal.
Pre-milking sanitizer	Helps reduce bacteria on udder and teats.
Paper towels	Keep a whole roll handy and use a fresh one for each doe.
Teat dip	Seals off teat ends to prevent infection.
Udder ointment	Keeps udders from getting chapped.

HANDLING MILK

Under normal conditions, milk is sterile inside a healthy mammary gland. But milk is an ideal medium for bacteria, and once it leaves the udder it's subject to contamination. Cooling milk to below 40°F within an hour of milking reduces the chances it will spoil. Refrigeration may not cool milk fast enough. It's better to place containers in circulating cold water, or in a bucket of ice water. If you get much over five gallons a day, consider acquiring a commercial water-immersion cooler or a bulk tank for sufficiently rapid cooling.

Goat milk contains the enzyme *caproic acid*, which causes it to go "goaty" with age. If you prefer raw milk, drink it fresh. Pasteurize stored milk to destroy elements that may alter its flavor, including bacteria. Pasteurizing is essential if you want to make good cheese. It involves heating the milk to a temperature that is balanced against the length of time it's kept hot.

For example, you can pasteurize at 145°F for thirty minutes, or at 163°F for thirty seconds. Use a double boiler or a pail set in a large pot of water to prevent scorching.

Pasteurized milk has a cooked flavor, which can be minimized by exact timing and rapid cooling. A small automatic, commercial home pasteurizer—using pressurized heat and vacuum sealed cooling for fast pasteurization without overheating—will give you the best flavor.

OFF-FLAVORED MILK

Flavor	Description	Possible causes
Oxidized	cardboardy; tallowy; metallic	Using brass, nickel, white-metal or tin milking equipment; doe's drinking water is high in iron or copper; milk exposed to sunlight.
Rancid	bitter; soapy	Individual trait; late lactation; changing the temperature of stored milk, such as adding warm milk to chilled milk.
Feed or weed flavor	sweet; aromatic	Sudden changes in feed; grass or corn silage; cabbage, turnip, garlic, and other strong vegetables; wild onion and other weeds; doe smelled strong odors.
Unclean flavor	goaty; barny	Dirty barn or animals; damp, strong odors; unclean milking equipment; milk left in barn too long.
Malty or acid flavor	grape-nut; sour	Unclean milking equipment; failure to cool to 40°F or below; too slow cooling.

From: John C. Porter, Dairy Goat Production Practices, FFT Series #20, Cooperative Extension Service, University of New Hampshire, Durham, NH.

GOING ON TEST

The National Cooperative Dairy Herd Improvement Association sponsors Dairy Herd Improvement (DHI) testing to establish accurate, reliable, and verifiable milking records for participating herds. The Dairy Herd Improvement Registry (DHIR) is the same program, in cooperation with a dairy goat registry. In addition to all the other services, it gives superior milkers recognition (*M) that becomes a permanent part of their registration information. Participation in either program may involve only the recording of milk yields, or it may include testing of milk samples for protein, fat, and other components, at your option.

This home pasteurizer uses pressurized heat and vacuum-sealed cooling for best flavor. (Photo courtesy of New England Cheesemakers Supply Co., Ashfield, Massachusetts)

Bucks also participate in the DHIR program, and receive distinction for the production of their ancestors (*B) and their offspring (+B).

Dairy management and health management plans are also available for additional fees, and so is direct access to your herd's records through a home computer terminal. If you're interested in going on test, your county Extension agent or state Dairy Specialist can tell you how.

A cream separator is handy if you make ice cream or butter. (Photo courtesy of New England Cheesemaking Supply Co., Ashfield, Massachusetts)

BUTTER AND CREAM

Because goat milk is naturally homogenized, the cream does not rise to the top as readily as it does in cow milk. If you want to separate it for whipping, or to make ice cream or butter, you'll need a hand-crank or electric cream separator. If you'd like to keep your household in homemade butter, you'll also need a hand-operated or electric churn. This equipment is fairly costly, but pays for itself if you're big on cream and butter.

Cream separated from goat milk is pure white, unlike the yellow-tinged cream from cow milk. You can get an idea what it's like if you refrigerate fresh milk in a container with a wide opening, until a thin layer forms on the top that can be skimmed off easily. Butter made from this cream is also white. If you prefer it yellow, you can purchase traditional or natural butter coloring from cheesemaking and dairy suppliers.

YOGURT

Some kinds of bacteria in milk are beneficial, such as those used to make yogurt, buttermilk, and cheese. Culturing milk both enhances its flavor and increases its keeping ability. In cultured milk products, lactose breaks down and becomes easier to digest. The beneficial bacteria also help maintain the natural bacterial balance in your stomach, and restore it after an illness or antibiotic treatment.

Yogurt is the most popular of all cultured milk products and is easy to make. Heat milk to 110°F and stir in two tablespoons per quart of your favorite yogurt starter, or a quarter-cup of unsweetened, unflavored store-bought yogurt. Place the cultured milk in a commercial yogurt maker for ten hours, or in a glass casserole dish in a warm place for several hours while it ferments and reaches the right consistency. When it's ready, the yogurt will retain the impression of a spoon pressed into its surface. At too low a temperature, yogurt takes longer to set up, becomes sour, and may separate out into curds and whey.

Refrigeration causes fermentation to stop and keeps the yogurt from getting too tart. It also enhances its keeping qualities, and creates a more refreshing dish. If you find the yogurt a little too thin, next time add some unflavored gelatin dissolved in cold water along with the culture. If you like your yogurt sweetened, add a bit of honey. Yogurt is terrific as a base for salad dressing, makes a great dessert with stewed or fresh fruit, and can be used to whip up summertime frozen yogurt treats.

CHEESE

You can make a quick and simple cheese spread from fresh yogurt by pouring it into a colander lined with cheesecloth. Tie up the four corners and hang it to drain until it stops dripping in about six hours. Salt to taste and refrigerate for use within a week. Vary the flavor by coating the spread with cracked pepper, adding garlic and Italian herbs, or mixing in some fresh dill or chives.

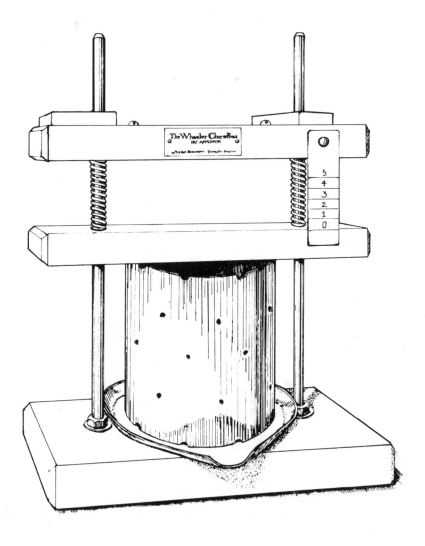

For well-shaped hard cheeses, you will need to make or buy a press such as this. (Photo courtesy of New England Cheesemaking Supply Co., Ashfield, Massachusetts)

Soft Cheese

An easy soft cheese can be made by using vinegar to coagulate the milk. Heat milk to 185°F. Slowly stir in about one tablespoon of vinegar per quart of milk until it begins to curdle, which sometimes takes a drop or two more vinegar. Drain through cheesecloth. Add three-quarters of a teaspoon of salt per original quart of milk. Drain two or three hours, then refrigerate. Two quarts of milk will make about three-quarters of a pound of this mild cheese.

Another mild cheese that's firm enough to slice requires combining warm milk with rennet, a natural enzyme that causes milk to coagulate. Rennet is available through cheesemaking suppliers and in some grocery and drug stores. Cool a gallon of pasteurized milk to 85°F and add a quarter tablet of rennet, dissolved in a little cool water. In about forty-five minutes to an hour, the milk will set up until, when you push your finger into it and lift up, it breaks clean. Using a long, thin knife, make a series of parallel slices to cut the curd into one-inch cubes. The watery part, or whey, will separate out and the coagulated milk, or curds, will fall to the bottom in about fifteen minutes. Drain off the whey (you can chill it as a drink or use it in cooking) and add one tablespoon of salt. Hang the curds in a piece of cheesecloth for a few hours until the dripping stops and the cheese becomes firm. This cheese is good crumbled in salads. If you soak it in salt water, it will taste quite similar to the Greek feta cheese.

Hard Cheese

With the same ingredients and a little more time, you can make a mild, hard cheese suitable for slicing or grating. Begin the same way, by cooling pasteurized milk to 85°F. This time use two gallons to get a two-pound chunk of cheese. Add the rennet as before, let the milk set up, and cut it into curds. Now the process begins to differ.

Stir the curds gently with your hand for fifteen minutes, breaking up any big pieces. Slowly heat the curds to 102°F, letting the temperature go up 1.5°F every five minutes for about an hour. When the curd holds its shape in your hand, but falls apart after a moment, turn off the heat. Continue stirring every ten minutes for about an hour until a pressed handful of curds can easily be shaken apart. Pour into a cheesecloth-lined colander, drain, and mix in two tablespoons of salt, a little at a time. Tie up the corners of the cheesecloth and hang to drain for about half an hour.

Remove the cheese from the cheesecloth and shape it into a patty no more than six inches across, pressing it with your hands to smooth out cracks. Wrap a cheesecloth bandage around the outside; then place four layers of cheesecloth each on the top and the bottom.

Now you must press the cheese. This can be done with two boards, weighted down with some bricks or a potful of water. Press about eight or ten hours, then turn the cheese and press another eight or ten hours. Remove the cheese from the press and let it dry a few hours until a crust forms. To keep it from drying further, dip it in melted paraffin. Store the cheese in a cool place, turning it occasionally and checking for mold. Wipe away any mold with a cloth dampened in salty water. The cheese will be ready to eat in about a month.

Other Varieties

Different varieties of cheese get their characteristic flavors by using appropriate cultures before adding the rennet. If you get into cheese-making, you'll probably want to make or buy a proper cheese press, and get cheesemaker's paraffin that's more pliable and does not crack as readily as household wax. There are books devoted to cheesemaking, and catalogs of supplies for making many kinds of cheese. Some of these resources are listed at the back of the book.

Chapter 10

UDDER CARE

The udder is a fairly delicate instrument that requires care to keep it in good working order. Because a doe is small and her udder hangs low, it is subject to injury—nursing kids butt against it, improper milking damages it, any abuse causes a breakdown in its internal workings and inhibits milk production.

Because udder care is important both to good milk production and the health of the doe, it pays to know how the udder works. It is divided into two halves, preferably about the same size and separated by a cleft. Its size depends on the size and age of the doe, her breeding, and how long she's been in milk. Strong ligaments, called *udder supports* or *attachments*, hold the udder to the abdominal wall. If the attachments weaken, the udder becomes pendulous, hanging long and low so that it's even more subject to injury.

UDDER'S INNER STRUCTURE

Alveoli (or acini)	The tiny secretory cells that are the basic units of the mammary system.
Lobules	Groups of alveoli bound together by a wall of connective tissue.
Lobes	Groups of lobules.
Myoepithelial cells	Muscular cells that surround the alveoli, responsible for the release of the hormone oxytocin that allows milk let-down.
Milk canals	Series of ductules and ducts that lead from the lobules and lobes to the udder cistern.
Udder cistern (or gland cistern)	Located just above each teat and capable of holding about a pound of milk.
Teat cistern	Reservoir between the udder cistern and the streak canal.
Streak canal	Final passageway out of the teat.
Fuerstenberg's rosette	Several folds of mucous membranes, each with secondary folds, that function as a plug and seal to prevent both milk leakage and bacterial entrance into the gland.

Based on: G. F. W. Haenlein and R. Caccese, "The Udder," in Extension Goat Handbook, Extension Service, USDA, 1984.

Each half of the udder contains a single mammary gland, within which are tiny cells that secrete milk. These are surrounded by muscular cells responsible for letting down the milk when kids nurse or you milk the doe. Most of the milk is stored in the inner structure of the udder until the doe is stimulated to let it down. Then it travels through a series of passageways and storage areas and finally comes squirting out the teat opening into the eager mouth of a hungry kid, or into an empty milk pail.

Regular milking at twelve-hour intervals, thorough washing and massaging of the udder prior to milking, proper milking technique including not pulling down on the teats or attempting to strip out every last drop, and using a teat dip and an udder balm, all help keep the udder working properly.

UDDER INJURY

The udder is especially subject to injury when a doe runs through brush to browse, is fenced with barbed wire, or encounters other objects on which she can easily bang or cut herself. Superficial cuts should be cleaned with warm, soapy water, dried, and coated with iodine. Deep wounds, ones that leak milk, or any on the teat itself, may need suturing for proper healing. A cut on the teat tends to break open every time you milk, inhibiting rapid healing. Until healing is complete, watch for signs of infection.

Cuts on the udder usually look worse than they really are because they bleed so profusely. Wipe the blood away and press with a clean towel to stem the bleeding. If the cut is deep enough to require veterinary assistance, avoid breaking the clot and causing renewed bleeding by keeping up the pressure until you get to the vet.

A heavy milker can be fitted with an udder support to protect her udder and teats from injury, and to relieve strained attachments.

MASTITIS

Mastitis is an inflammation of the udder caused by one of several different organisms, all treated in different ways. To determine what is causing the problem requires a culture test of the milk. Periodic milk analyses may reveal the presence of mastitis when no symptoms are visible.

Mastitis can be either acute or chronic. In acute cases, a doe acts sick, runs a fever, and her udder becomes hot and swollen on one or both sides. The milk may become thick, chunky, ropy, or bad smelling. Acute mastitis is caused by injury or insect stings that stress the udder and allow bacteria to multiply within it. Low-hanging udders are particularly susceptible.

After a doe has had acute mastitis, some bacteria may remain in her udder, trapped by scar tissue and waiting for a chance to start up again. Therefore, incomplete or improper treatment of acute mastitis can lead to a chronic case. The doe will not look sick, but may occasionally give abnormal milk. Her udder may swell up, though it won't be hot or hard. You may feel lumps of hardened tissue masses inside the udder. Once a veterinarian or diagnostic lab has determined the cause and recommended treatment for acute mastitis, follow it to the letter, continuing to the end of the prescribed treatment even when it seems the problem has cleared up.

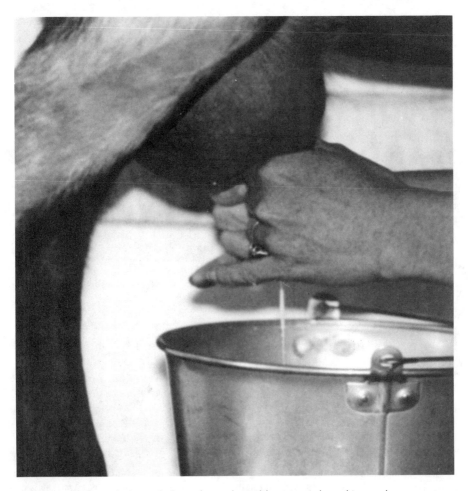

Proper milking techniques help to keep the udder in good working order. (Photo by Matto)

Prevention

Good sanitation and strict cleanliness help prevent mastitis. If you suspect it in your herd, milk first fresheners first, healthy does next, and does suspected of having mastitis last to avoid spreading infection. Follow a regular program of teat dipping to seal the teat canals from infection. Change the dip after each doe. If you're trying to control a bout of mastitis, change dips after each teat of each doe. See that your facilities are properly designed to prevent banging of udders. Be sure that your milking technique is correct.

Detection

You can routinely test your does with the California Mastitis Test (CMT), available through dairy suppliers and many feed stores. The CMT checks for *leucocytes*, a type of somatic cell. Somatic cells are body cells that are normally present in small quantities in milk. Leucocytes, in particular, are white blood cells that develop as a defense against infection, or as a result of irritation due to improper milking or some health-related stress condition. Goat milk—and human milk, but not cow milk—also contains numerous pieces of small, harmless mammary tissue called *cytoplasmic particles*. Most tests include these in the somatic cell count, giving a false impression that infection may be present. The CMT is a widely used home test that distinguishes between leucocytes and cytoplasmic particles.

DRYING OFF AND FRESHENING

When a doe begins a lactation period, she is said to *freshen*. Freshening usually requires the stimulation of kidding, but on occasion a young doe will spontaneously come into milk before she is bred. In this case, she is called a *maiden milker* or a *virgin milker*.

Sometimes when a doe freshens, her udder will be tight and hard, one of the many conditions that is believed to be preventable by heat-treating all colostrum and milk fed to doelings from birth. When a doe freshens with a hard udder, work out the tightness with deep massaging and warm compresses. It may take several days, or even a few weeks, before the udder becomes pliable again.

Around ten months after freshening, or perhaps sooner, many does dry off naturally. Others have to be deliberately dried off before being freshened. A heavy milker may never dry off completely. A good producing doe may give milk for two years or more before needing to be freshened to renew production.

With the right bloodlines, then, it's possible to breed does every two years to obtain milk without producing unwanted kids. On the other hand, the doe's yield will decrease with time, and she may dry off well before freshening is possible next season. You may end up feeding a dry doe for several months longer than you anticipated. It's a chance you take when trying to extend the lactation period.

When a doe fails to dry off naturally two months before she's due to kid, you'll have to help her out. If she's giving less than three pounds a day, simply reduce the number of milkings to one a day, then every

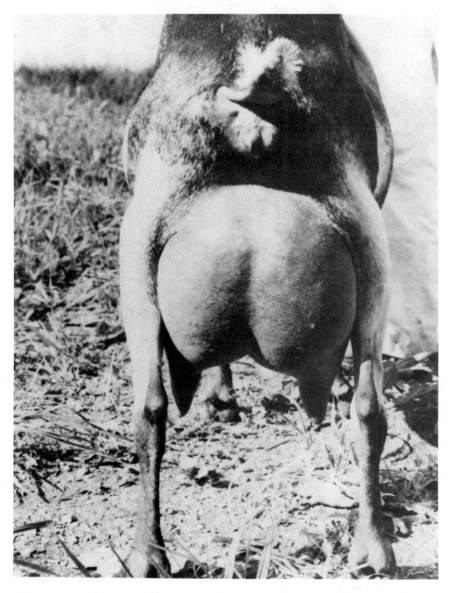

Does with outstanding udders like this Alpine's pass on their genes through semen collection from their sons for artificial insemination.
(Photo courtesy of Earth Dance Alpines, Ligonier, Pennsylvania, and Magnum Semen Works, Hampstead, Maryland)

other day, then none. If the udder continues to swell, milk her out again about a week after her last milking. Some swelling of the udder is necessary, as the pressure helps stop the milk flow more quickly. Heavy milkers may be harder to dry off. Abruptly stopping to milk can cause udder irritation and damage. Instead, reduce the doe's grain ration, decrease her water intake, and change her routine to help her dry off more quickly. Continue teat dipping for one or two weeks after you stop milking to seal the teat ends.

UDDER EVALUATION	
Degree of Seriousness	**Defect**
Moderate	Teats —Too close together; bulbous; very large or small; pointed outward; uneven in size; hard to milk; not clearly separated from udder.
Serious	Teats —Leaking. Udder—Pendulous; too distended to determine texture; one side less than half the size of the other.
Very serious	Teats —Double orifice; extra teats; teats cut off. Udder—Lacks size and capacity relative to doe's size.
Depends on degree problem	Udder—Lacks front, rear, or side attachments; separation between udder halves; scar tissue; beefy udder.
Disqualification	Teats —Blind teat; double teat; extra teat that interferes with milking. Udder—Half not functioning; active mastitis; abnormal milk.

Based on: Byrin E. Colby, et al, Dairy Goats: Breeding/Feeding Management, American Dairy Goat Association, 1972.

Dry Period Treatment

The dry period is a good time to treat for lice, since you won't have to worry about getting pesticides into the milk. When a doe has had mastitis during the preceding lactation, treat her with a dry cow mastitis preparation. A cow's udder has four quarters instead of two halves. Infuse each half of the doe's udder with the dosage designed for a cow's quarter udder. Seeing that your does freshen in the peak of health ensures that they produce quality milk in the next lactation.

Chapter 11

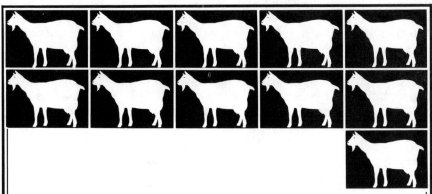

HEALTH CARE

If you take good care of your goats and are careful not to track in diseases from other herds, chances are good you'll have few health problems. But if you enjoy bringing home new goats, frequently visit other herds, or show your animals, you're likely to have problems sooner or later. It's not that other people's goats are less healthy than yours. But bringing yours together with others provides the opportunity for a trade of infectious organisms that might not exist in your herd, and to which your goats therefore may not have immunity. The excitement and stress of showing make an animal even more susceptible. It helps to isolate show returnees and newcomers for at least a month, and watch for signs of disease. Problems are less likely if you don't let your herd get too big too fast, stretching thin your management skills, time, and facilities.

Avoid indiscriminate use of medications, including wormers and pesticides. Overusing drugs may mean that your goats will fail to respond when treatment really becomes necessary. In addition, a condition may get worse if you use the wrong treatment. Never administer a drug unless you're certain what problem you're treating. Many diseases have nearly identical symptoms and require laboratory examination of feces or body fluids for positive identification. Be sure that any preparation you use is safe for dairy animals and will not affect milk. If you need to use a milk-affecting remedy, keep accurate records so you'll know when milk use is safe again.

HEALTH CHECKS

Be familiar with the common goat problems so you can act quickly if they appear in your herd. Spend time every day looking over each animal. Notice the shape, color, and texture of feces. Be alert for changes in barn odor. Watch for changes in the way each animal eats and moves. Skin and hair conditions are good indications of health. The coat should be smooth and the skin pliable. Milk is also a good health indicator. It should be sweet, pure white, free of odor, and flow freely without lumps or stringy masses.

Keep a record of normal vital signs for every goat in your herd so you'll be able to detect any abnormality, since each individual animal differs slightly from the norm.

NORMAL VITAL STATISTICS

Lifespan, average	— 8 to 10 years
maximum	— 30 years
Pulse	— 70 to 80 beats per minute
Rectal temperature	— 101.5° to 104°F
Respiratory rate	— 12 to 20 per minute
Rumination	— 1 to 1.5 per minute

TEMPERATURE

Among the data in your records should be the normal temperature for each goat. Take the temperature two or three different times to be sure you have an accurate reading, and write down your findings so that during an emergency you won't have to rely on memory. Whenever a goat seems sick, the first thing you should do is take its temperature. If you call a vet, be ready to say what that temperature is. After you start treatment, keep track of the temperature to determine if the goat is getting better.

The best time to take a goat's temperature is early in the morning, when the animal is at rest. Use a rectal thermometer designed specifically for livestock. Have the goat restrained in a stanchion, or crowd it against a solid wall with your knee. Lubricate the thermometer and shake it down until it reads 100°F or less. Grasp the tail and slowly insert the themometer into the rectum about two inches deep. A conventional mercury thermometer will take around three minutes. An electronic one will record the temperature in mere seconds, and some beep to let you know when the correct reading has been reached. Wash and disinfect the thermometer after each use.

Temperature Variations

The temperature of a healthy goat varies, rising slightly throughout the day and falling again at night. It is also influenced by the reproductive cycle. During estrus, a doe's temperature may rise, then drop a degree or so just before ovulation. During the first half of pregnancy, her temperature may be slightly above normal.

A goat's temperature is also influenced by season. Wintertime rectal temperatures may be one to two degrees below summer levels. Extended exposure to warm or humid weather causes a rise in body temperature, especially since a goat's coat inhibits its ability to lose heat, and goats don't sweat much. If water is restricted during hot weather, dehydration will lead to a further decrease in ability to sweat, and fever may result. This type of fever is easy to treat. Simply supply plenty of drinking water.

Fever due to hot weather may also cause imbalance in a goat's digestive acid-to-base ratio, or its water-to-salt use, leading to *acidosis* — the lowering of rumen pH so that the animal becomes more susceptible to enterotoxemia. Goats should always have free access to baking soda and loose mineral salt. Both are especially important during summer weather.

Fever may also result from infectious diseases. In acute infection, temperature remains high. In chronic cases, it may come down during the night. Extended periods of fever may lead to convulsions, which in turn further increase the body heat. Convulsions may be controlled with cool water soaks, sedatives, or anesthetics. A goat cannot survive a body temperature more than ten degrees above its norm.

Low temperatures may result from extended exposure to cold or from injury leading to shock. Shivering helps bring the temperature back up. Using a heater or electric pad to raise body temperature slowly may help. A very low temperature probably means that the goat is dying from shock, exposure, or other causes.

Variations in the body temperature of kids are greater than in mature goats, and their temperture runs higher in response to infection. Very old goats may experience little change in temperature no matter how serious an infection may be. To further complicate things, temperature goes up with exercise, excitement, and rumen fermentation, sometimes throwing doubts on the meaningfulness of the rectal temperature of a particular animal. Taking the temperature of other goats in the herd and comparing your findings to the norm for each will help you learn whether outside factors may be affecting the temperature of the goat you're concerned about.

ORAL MEDICATION

Oral medication is usually used for digestive problems, diarrhea, worms, and bacterial infections. Liquid medication is called a *drench*, and administering it is called *drenching*. Stand over the goat, facing the same direction, with one leg on each side. Press your knees against the animal to keep it in place. If the goat is skittish, have someone help you or tie it down. Insert a drench-filled syringe or the neck of a plastic bottle — never glass — into the side of the mouth. Do not restrict its tongue, or the goat will not be able to swallow. Pour in the medication slowly to avoid choking or getting fluid into the lungs and causing pneumonia. Don't lift the animal's head, or choking may result. Stop if the goat struggles, and resume only after it calms down.

A large pill given to goats and other livestock is called a *bolus*. Devices called *balling guns* are designed to get the bolus behind the tongue so the animal can't spit it out. Greasing the bolus with shortening helps it slide down easily, giving the goat little chance to struggle against swallowing. Some pills can be broken into halves or thirds for easier swallowing without choking.

When a goat is vomiting or scouring, it may not be able to keep down oral medication long enough to do any good. A shot then becomes necessary.

INJECTIONS

Some medications can only be administered by injection. There are several different ways to give a shot, depending on the type of medication being used. Injecting a drug by the wrong method can cause problems, or even kill a goat. *Subcutaneous* shots put medication just under the skin where it is absorbed slowly. *Intramuscular* injections allow more rapid absorption. *Intravenous* shots that get drugs directly into the bloodstream are sometimes necessary to save a goat's life, but administering them requires extreme skill. A variety of other types of injections are used for special treatments.

DAIRY GOAT INJECTIONS

Type	Location	Purpose
Subcutaneous (subcut)	Under loose skin on neck, flank, withers, or elbow	Slow, sustained absorption.
Intramuscular (IM)	Muscle of hindquarters or side of neck	Rapid absorption.
Intravenous (IV)	Jugular vein, milk vein	Very rapid absorption into blood stream. (Requires experience and skill.)
Intraperitoneal (IP)	Abdominal cavity on right side in hollow near hip	Slow, sustained absorption. (Requires experience and skill.)
Intradermal	Between skin layers in caudal fold of tail	TB testing.
Intraruminal	Rumen at left flank	Administer anti-foaming agent for bloat.
Intramammary	Udder	Treat for mastitis

Successful injections of any type require knowledge of the exact location of muscles, nerves, and blood veins, as well as complete restraint of the goat. Needles and syringes must be sterile. Disposable ones are cheap and are far easier, safer, and less time-consuming than trying to sterilize them after each use. Before administering any injection, part or clip back the hair, wash the skin, and clean it with an antiseptic. After inserting the needle, but before injecting the medication, withdraw the plunger. See that no fluids enter it and, except for an intravenous shot, that blood is not drawn. If you have no experience giving shots, have a knowledgeable goatkeeper or a veterinarian help you until you feel confident.

In addition to the occasional medical treatment, your goats will need regular vaccinations and possibly worming shots. An annual tetanus booster is an absolute must, especially if your animals tend to wound themselves regularly or if horses are, or have been, pastured nearby. Horses are natural carriers of the organism that causes tetanus, and goats are very susceptible to picking it up through deep cuts or punctures commonly caused by nails and stiff wire. Other injections you may need to give are enterotoxemia shots and selenium shots.

ROUTINE HEALTH MAINTENANCE

A good goat-oriented veterinarian can help you evaluate your area, as well as your method of herd management, to work out a reliable health-care program. It's a good idea to find a vet who knows goats, and establish rapport so you'll have someone to turn to and trust in times of medical emergency.

But such emergencies will be few and far between if you arm yourself with a basic knowledge of goat health and disease, and incorporate into your herd management plan a solid program of routine preventive care.

Chapter 12

TROUBLE SHOOTING

ABSCESSES (BOILS)

Abscesses are common in goats and can occur just about anywhere on, or in, the body. Some disappear on their own. Others are serious, especially if they're internal or on the udder. Occasional abscesses may be caused by injury, improperly given shots, foreign matter under the skin, or infected cuts. They are not contagious. Other types of abscesses may be highly contagious and the inexperienced person should not try to treat them. Repeated occurrence of abscesses on a goat, or in a herd, should be discussed with a vet.

You can treat the occasional abscess, provided it is not on the throat or udder where it may lie close to a blood vessel. Let the abscess come to a head. Then isolate the goat to prevent spreading infection, and draw off some of the fluid with a needle and syringe. If it looks bloody, leave the abscess alone or you may bleed your goat to death. If the fluid looks more like pus, trim the hair from around the lump. Wash the surface with warm, soapy water, rinse with clear water, and pat dry. Wearing rubber gloves and using a sharp sterilized blade, make an incision at the base of the lump where the pus will easily drain away. Collect the pussy contents in a paper towel, clear out the wound with a cotton stick, and burn both to prevent spreading the problem. Clean the wound with warm, soapy water, rinse with clear water, pat dry, and squirt in a little antibiotic. Clean the wound daily while it heals.

BUCK PROBLEMS

Bucks may become infertile through injury from their housing or fighting with other bucks. Prevention involves removing injury-causing protrusions in the facilities and separating aggressive animals.

A buck may develop crystallized stones in his bladder or urethra, making urination painful or impossible. The usual cause is repeated eating of leaves from beets, mustard, Swiss chard, or rhubarb.

DIARRHEA

Causes of diarrhea are eating too much grain in proportion to other roughage, a sudden shift to lush pasture, grazing after the first frost, worms, poisoning, or coccidiosis. Curing diarrhea may simply require gradually increasing fiber feeds. Worms and poisoning are discussed elsewhere in this chapter.

Coccidiosis is more likely in kids than in adult goats. Thinness, loss of appetite, and bloody diarrhea are all symptoms, and so is sudden death. Coccidiosis is caused by a protozoa and is diagnosed by taking a fecal sample to the vet. Control involves good sanitation and preventing wet conditions. Other causes of diarrhea in kids are discussed in chapter 8 on kid care.

DIGESTIVE UPSET

Overeating of grass or grains may cause indigestion. It usually occurs when goats find their way into the grain bin and gorge themselves, or when a herd is let into legume pasture in spring and chows down. Make sure goats have access to plenty of hay before they graze lush pasture. At the beginning of the pasture season, get them used to green feed gradually by cutting it for them daily before turning them out on their own.

Both lush legumes and excess grain cause gas to form that a goat cannot belch up, so instead it bloats up. Sometimes a drench of one cup of vegetable or mineral oil will help move the feed through more quickly and slow the bloating. Massaging the stomach area and keeping the goat on its feet and moving around also help break up gas. In extreme cases, it may be necessary to use a stomach tube or a device to puncture the rumen and relieve gas pressure, but often when things have gone that far, the animal never recovers its full potential.

Enterotoxemia, caused by an organism related to the one that causes tetanus, may result from overeating. When goats stuff themselves on feeds that are high in starch, and the rumen ferments too quickly, its pH drops. If the pH falls below 4.8, a condition called *acidosis* develops. The lower pH encourages rapid multiplication of natural bacteria in the digestive tract. In the process, potent toxins are released, and *enterotoxemia* is the result. Symptoms are depression, appearance of intoxication, incoordination, convulsions, coma, and death. In kids, sudden death may be the first sign.

Enterotoxemia can be avoided by feeding at least twice a day so goats don't get overly hungry and stuff themselves at the first opportunity. Make any ration changes gradually over a ten-day to three-week period, depending on how drastic the change is. Vaccination offers protection that is transferred from a mother to her kids through colostrum. There is also good evidence that sunflower seeds in the diet of dairy goats helps prevent enterotoxemia.

EARS

If your goat shakes its head, scratches its ears, or carries its head to one side, or you find crusty material and waxy buildup in the ears, the problem is probably ear mites. Treat with the same miticide you would use on a cat or dog, or gently massage a little mineral oil into the ear. Adding one part rotenone to three parts mineral oil will help kill the mites.

Since mites spread quickly from one goat to another, treat the whole herd at the same time. Mites carry certain infectious diseases, so be sure eradication is complete by repeating treatment weekly for at least six weeks.

EYES

Runny eyes may be a sign of colds or pneumonia. If the eyes are red around the edges and tears flow, *pinkeye* is probably the problem. Pinkeye is a contagious infection that can spread from one goat to another. In extreme cases, it causes blindness. It usually occurs in hot, dry weather, is spread by flies, and is aggravated by wind and dust. Treat with antibiotic ointment. All goats in the herd should be treated at the same time, even those showing no symptoms.

FREEZING

Kids are usually born during cold months, making their ears and feet susceptible to freezing. The first sign is stiffness, sometimes leading to swelling. The affected parts will be tender and feel hot. Untreated, the animal may lose the use of these parts, requiring amputation, and will rarely do well as a dairy animal.

Ensure that your does do not kid outdoors during winter. Take them into a stall in plenty of time. Prevent freezing by heating the kidding stall up to 40°F. As soon as the kids become active, gradually reduce the heat until the ambient temperature is reached.

If a kid has been frozen, take it inside and place it in a tub of warm, not hot, water. Soak the kid for fifteen minutes, then dry it thoroughly, using towels and a blow dryer. Keep the kid in a warm place in a clean box padded with dry towels. Talk to your vet about the need for cortisone injections to increase circulation and reduce swelling and pain, and about antibiotics as protection against infection.

Guard against frostbite in kids by confining a doe to her stall as her time nears. (Photo by Matto)

JOINT SWELLING (ARTHRITIS)

A common problem in goats is puffy and painful joints. Swollen knees may be the result of injury, as indicated by soft puffiness. If the joint is hard and calcified, the cause is more likely to be arthritis. Non-viral forms of arthritis are caused by bacteria, mycoplasmas, and chlamydiae, and are treated with antibiotics. Usual indications are depression, high temperature, and hot joints. A sample of fluids from the joint can be cultured to determine what organism is responsible and what treatment should be used. Some vets are not very knowledgeable about this sort of test, and some organisms are hard to detect.

In the early 70s, researchers at Washington State University identified the *Caprine Arthritis Encephalitis (CAE) virus* responsible for arthritic conditions and a whole host of other problems including pneumonia and infected udder at freshening. It is believed that the virus is not very contagious, but at the time of discovery the majority of American dairy goats had been infected as kids through their mothers' milk. Best known control is to heat all colostrum and milk fed to kids, as described in chapter 8 on kid care. You can also have your herd blood-tested periodically to identify and cull carriers.

LAMENESS

Lameness may be due to broken bones, which can usually be mended. Sometimes the only symptom is that the goat refuses to use a leg. Other times you may see the broken bone pressing against the skin or even sticking out. Broken bones are most often caused by mismanagement—a goat gets tangled in a fence or is hit by a car. If a bone breaks, try to keep the animal from thrashing around and causing itself further damage. Move the goat to a vet as carefully as possible to keep the bone from breaking through the skin, which may lead to infection. After a cast has been applied, keep the animal away from mud and rain. Check daily for swelling of the leg, dampness, off-odors, and coldness in the foot. At the first sign of problems, return the goat to the vet to prevent loss of the leg. Mending takes about six weeks in an adult, three weeks for a kid.

Foot rot also causes lameness, as well as pain, bad odor, and a grey cheesy discharge. It occurs where harmful fungi thrive in wet and muddy conditions with poor air circulation. Because dairy goats are usually kept in dry housing and have their hooves trimmed regularly, hoof rot is rarely a problem. Treatment involves trimming away the rotted area and applying a 10 to 30 percent copper sulfate solution. If your whole herd is affected, your vet may recommend placing a medicated footbath where the goats will walk through it regularly.

Lameness is also caused by overgrown hooves, as described in chapter 5, where details on hoof trimming techniques are given.

MOUTH SORES

Scabs around a goat's mouth may indicate the contagious disease *soremouth*—or *contagious ecthymia*—caused by a virus that remains in the soil for long periods of time. Sometimes the sores appear on the feet as well. The disease lasts from one to four weeks and spreads rapidly from goat to goat. It is not serious in adults, but it keeps kids from eating properly, and if they're nursing, they can infect the doe's udder and make it painful. Remove scabby material with hydrogen peroxide and gauze, then cover the infected area with zinc oxide. Work gently, wearing plastic gloves to keep from getting infected yourself. The goal of treatment is to prevent secondary bacterial infection.

Once a herd has had a bout of soremouth, all those goats are immune for life. A vaccine may be used after kids are weaned, but it is a live vaccine that will bring the infection to your herd if it wasn't there before. The vaccine is more often used to get rid of the disease once it appears in a herd.

POISONING

Goats may be poisoned any number of ways, all of which result from mismanagement. They may chew or lick walls, fences, or stalls painted with lead base paint, causing weakness, staggering, and diarrhea. Urea, a natural compound used as a protein substitute in many dairy mixes, is also toxic to goats if too much is fed too rapidly.

CAE-free does may safely nurse their kids. (Photo by Matto)

Plants are perhaps the chief source of poisoning. Non-toxic plants may be made poisonous with pesticide sprays. Ornamental shrub prunings tossed into the goat yard are another source of poisoning. So are home mixed feeds inadvertently containing chopped toxic vegetation that can't be sorted out by the goats. Some plants are poisonous only at certain times of year, others are always so. For many plants—wild cherry and oak included—toxic substances become concentrated in the wilted leaves, to which goats are unfortunately attracted. In some areas, it's necessary to prevent browsing during autumn when these withered leaves pile up on the ground. Since goats nibble a little here and a little there, they are otherwise rarely affected by poisonous plants unless moved to an area where they're unfamiliar with the vegetation, extreme hunger forces them to browse on toxic plants, or the only available browse consists of poisonous vegetation. The toxic evergreen mountain laurel, for instance, becomes attractive to goats in winter when most other vegetation has died back.

Goats are less subject to plant poisoning than other types of livestock, and are sometimes used to browse down toxic vegetation before other animals are let in. Older goats become familiar with poisonous plants and learn to avoid them. Younger ones are more likely to get into trouble unless led by an experienced animal. There is no comprehensive list of plants that are poisonous specifically to goats. Many published lists are compilations of vegetation known to be toxic to other ruminants. Since vegetation varies from area to area, check with an experienced goatkeeper or a goat-loving veterinarian about local plants that may cause problems for your browsing herd.

Symptoms of poisoning are vomiting, frothing, staggering, cries for help, rapid or labored breathing, altered pulse, trembling, convulsions, and sudden death. The skin of white goats may be made sensitive to sunlight by certain plants. If you realize early enough that a goat has been poisoned, you can induce it to vomit the toxic substances with a drink of warm salty water, or a couple of tablespoons of salt on the back of the tongue.

RESPIRATORY PROBLEMS

Goats are particularly susceptible to respiratory problems, and this is one of the reasons they require protection from drafts and wet weather. In addition, lungworm infestation—indicated by rapid shallow breathing and coughing during exercise—may lead to pneumonia if untreated. Pneumonia may also result if the shelter is too warm or has no circulating fresh air, or too much humidity is allowed to build up in the air. Sudden changes in the weather or in feed cause stress that may lead to pneumonia. So does harassment from dogs or being moved to new quarters. Pneumonia-damaged lungs limit a goat's breathing capacity so that it becomes less aggressive, eats less, and fails to produce well.

Signs of pneumonia are puffing for breath, depression, lack of appetite, lying down more than usual, and sometimes coughing. A high temperature means the situation is serious. Treatment depends on the type of pneumonia.

Heat-treating all colostrum and milk fed to kids eliminates one cause of pneumonia, the *Caprine Arthritis Encephalitis virus*. Other methods of prevention include keeping stress to a minimum, ensuring cleanliness and good ventilation in housing, and isolating incoming animals until you're sure they are healthy.

SKIN CONDITIONS

Saanens and other white-skinned goats are subject to sunburn, most often after browsing plants that cause sensitivity to sunlight. Eating too much lush growth, especially ladino, white, or alsike clover, buckwheat, or rape, may cause sunburn or sloughing off of any white skinned areas on any breed.

Cuts and other wounds most commonly appear on the udder, but do occur on other parts of the body. For wounds that are not bad enough to require stitching, clip the hair back, wash with warm, soapy water, rinse with clear water, and disinfect with vet-strength (7 percent) iodine or other antiseptic. Leaving the cut open to air speeds healing. A tetanus antitoxin shot is a good precaution whenever a goat is wounded, even if it has already had a yearly booster. Keep the wound clean until healing is complete.

Ringworm is a common skin infection having nothing to do with worms. It is caused by a fungus that creates a crusty circle, usually on the goat's face or neck. It occurs most often in late winter when goats are kept indoors, and usually clears up when the animals get back outside as weather warms. Ringworm may be treated by softening the crust with warm, soapy water, removing it, patting the area dry, and applying iodine. Always work from the outside toward the center to prevent spread of the fungus.

Mange is caused by mites. It sometimes resembles a fungal infection, but is treated differently. It may take a skin scraping to tell the difference. *Sarcoptic mange* usually affects the neck, face, and belly, causing thickening of the skin and scratching. Clip or shave the affected area, wash it to remove loose skin and scabs, and apply a mange remedy to destroy the mites that have burrowed into the skin. *Demodex mange* is more common, usually occurring around the flanks and udder where you can feel small welts. Open the pustules and clean out the demodex mite with hydrogen peroxide. Poor nutrition, sanitation, and internal parasites all increase a goat's susceptibility to mites.

Lice, ticks, flies, and mosquitoes are other external parasites that plague goats, especially during spring and summer. Lice can also be a serious problem during the winter, when they multiply fast on a goat's long winter coat. Lice cause itching and irritation, and, if left unchecked, suck a goat's blood until anemia develops. If an animal rubs or scratches, and you see dandruff or patchy bald spots where it's been rubbing, lice are usually the problem. Use a louse powder according to label directions, treating the whole herd at the same time.

A smooth, clean coat like the one on this proud caramel Pygmy buck is a sign of good health. (Photo courtesy of Dewey Meadow Farms, Rome, New York)

WORMS

When goats browse more than they graze, they avoid picking up internal parasites from the ground. Lack of cleanliness, close confinement, and eating off the ground or bedding are the chief causes of infestation. Keeping goats off marshy or dewy pasture and rotating their forage area provide some control. Worms interfere with nutrition and reduce milk flow. Signs of infestation are listlessness, weight loss, rough coat, and sometimes diarrhea. The blood-sucking varieties also cause anemia.

A twice-yearly fecal sample consisting of about a dozen pellets from various animals, taken in a clean jar to your vet or nearest diagnostic laboratory, will tell you what type of worms are a problem in your herd and what treatment is necessary. In some areas, particularly where it's warm and humid, a regular worming schedule is required. Its goal should be to reduce internal parasites rather than eliminate them, since worm-free goats are susceptible to devastating infestations if they later become exposed. Regular worming may include treatment in the fall at the end of the pasture season, and again each spring a few weeks after kidding.

Chapter 13

ADDITIONAL GOATKEEPING BENEFITS

SHOWING

Summer shows are important in the lives of many goatkeepers. Those who have goats for fun or for family milk attend shows to meet others with the same interests, exchange information and ideas, and locate distributors for supplies and publications. To those for whom goat herding is a business, showing becomes a form of publicity. Consistently winning in large classes creates a demand for surplus stock.

Shows are sponsored by county and state fair associations and by local and state goat clubs. Many are sanctioned by registries including American Dairy Goat Association (ADGA), American Goat Society (AGS), International Dairy Goat Registry (IDGR), and the National

Pygmy Goat Association (NPGA). Shows are sanctioned when the registry approves the chosen judges, who are usually trained in programs sponsored by the registry in question. The names of winners go on permanent record with the registry. Prizes may be awarded in the form of ribbons, trophies, and sometimes small amounts of cash.

If you plan to show your goats, get a copy of the standard for the breeds you raise, to be sure your goats approach what is considered ideal, and have no defects. It also helps to attend a few shows to get an idea what it's all about. It's discouraging to enter a favorite animal, only to have it disqualified for some overlooked feature.

Goats aren't taken straight from the barn to the show-ring. They're first trained so they'll know what to expect and how to act, then groomed to look their best. If the finest goat in the world enters the

A 4-H youth trains her Oberhasli to stand calmly and squarely.
(Photo by Matto)

show-ring poorly trained and out of condition, the judge will not be able to give it fair consideration in comparison to calm, proud, well-groomed animals. Training and conditioning take time and patience. Neither can be accomplished overnight.

Training involves teaching the animal to walk around a show-ring with poise, respond to your lead, and stand with its front feet directly beneath it and back legs slightly spread. The goat must learn not to crowd animals ahead of it in the ring, and to accept your lead from both the right and left side, since you'll need to move around to keep the goat between you and the judge.

Conditioning requires getting your goat into the peak of health with its hooves well trimmed and its coat clipped and neat. Keep the goat on fresh, dry bedding up until the moment it enters the show-ring. Some exhibitors polish their animals just before their class is called, rubbing the coat with a towel or brush, cleaning off the hooves, and applying udder ointment.

It's traditional for dairy goat exhibitors to wear white during a show. In fact, youth groups, including 4-H and FFA, hold showmanship competitions in which the exhibitors themselves are judged for appearance as well as their abilities to handle and condition their goats. Attending such a competition will give you a good introduction to correct showing procedure.

Exhibition classes are usually divided by breed, then by age and by sex. There are sometimes also special classes such as market wethers, or get-of-sire—a specified number of kids from the same buck. Some pretty imaginative classes have been developed over the years. Study the premium book published by the sponsors of each show to see which classes your goats qualify for.

When a clerk calls your class, you will take your goat into a ring where the judge will look it over, along with all the others in the class. The judge will ask the exhibitors to change their order until the animals are arranged according to how closely each conforms to the standard. Then the judge will explain why each animal was placed as it was, and awards will be passed out. There may be time afterwards to ask questions about the scoring.

Unfortunately, each registry has its own pet scoring emphasis. As you become experienced at showing, you will learn to choose your entries according to which registry sanctions the show. All registries recognize permanent defects and disabilities that represent deviations from the ideal dairy goat. Serious defects, features that affect productivity or have a high degree of heritability, lead to disqualification. Defects and disqualifications may also pertain to the characteristics that make each breed unique, including color, shape, weight, and size. Sometimes a

TYPICAL JUDGES' SCORECARD

Category	Doe	Buck
GENERAL APPEARANCE: Attractive individuality revealing vigor; femininity/masculinity with a harmonious blending and correlation of parts; impressive style and attractive carriage, graceful/powerful walk. (Scored according to individual breed characteristics and color.)	30%	45%
DAIRY CHARACTER: Animation, angularity, general openness and freedom from excess tissue, with due regard to period of lactation for does. (Scored according to shape and condition of specific body parts.)	20%	30%
BODY CAPACITY: Relatively large in proportion to the size of the animal, providing ample digestive capacity, strength, and vigor. (Scored according to barrel and heart girth development.)	20%	25%
MAMMARY SYSTEM: A capacious, strongly attached well-carried udder of good quality, indicating heavy production and a long period of of usefulness. (Scored according to shape, capacity, attachment, and texture of the udder, and size and shape of the teats.)	30%	---
Highest Possible Score	100%	100%

Based on: American Dairy Goat Association Guidebook, 1985.

trait considered only a fault in a doe will disqualify a buck, because he has the potential of producing a greater number of offspring.

Most states have health regulations related to showing dairy goats. If your potential prizewinner develops a cough, runny nose or eyes, diarrhea, or any other adverse condition while you're preparing for a show, leave it home. Better to suffer the disappointment of not showing this time around than risk having a really sick goat, exposing others to whatever it's got, and experiencing the embarrassment of being asked to remove your goat from the showroom.

Any animal you bring home from a show should be isolated for at least ten days since it may have been exposed to incubating or airborne diseases. Watch especially for respiratory infections.

Patient training and good condition won a top prize for this Pygmy buck. (Photo courtesy of Dewey Meadows Farm, Rome, New York)

FERTILIZER

The manure of well-fed dairy goats is high in fertilizer value, and is excellent for garden vegetables, fruit trees, and ornamentals. A goat will deposit some 2 to 6 percent of its body weight in goat berries every day, and 1 to 4 percent of its body weight in urine. Exact amounts depend on how much the goat eats and drinks, and whether it loses fluids through perspiration or lactation.

When goats are foraging, much of this valuable resource goes to fertilize pastureland or is lost, but a significant portion can be recovered from bedding in the shelter. Thick, absorbent bedding soaks up and saves urine, which contains some 50 percent of the excreted nitrogen and around 65 percent of the potassium.

Soiled bedding from confined goats may amount to one and a half tons per animal per year, with an estimated N-P-K (Nitrogen–Phosphorus–Potassium) value of 1.3–1.5–0.4, varying with the type of bedding and its ratio to manure and urine. If you compost this bedding, keep it covered so rain won't leach out its fertilizing value.

GOAT MEAT

One of the facts of life for any dairy goatkeeper is dealing with surplus bucklings and aging does. Yet goats are not considered a serious source of meat in the United States as they are in other countries, including areas of the Mediterranean, the West Indies, and Africa.

Goat meat has a flavor all its own, and, like any flavor, it's hard to describe in words. Young goat tastes a bit like veal, and the meat from nearly mature animals is similar to grass-fed beef or fine venison. Goat meat is high in protein and low in calories, being lean and lacking the marbling associated with beef. Breed, age, sex, and method of processing all affect tenderness. In the East, goat meat is called *chevon*, and most commonly comes from wethers raised to about eighty pounds. In the West, it's called *cabrito*, and is usually the meat of kids two or three months old. Meat from older goats is called *chivo* or *mutton*.

Since goat is not unlike other types of more familiar meat, it can be cooked in the same ways. Few American cookbooks contain recipes specifically for goat meat, but cookbooks from Greece and other Mediterranean countries, as well as those on African and West Indian cookery, usually include delicious recipes that bring out its intrinsic qualities.

Very young kids may be butchered, dressed, and cooked like rabbit. At weaning, they're skinned and cleaned like any small animal, and are usually quartered or left whole and roasted over coals on a spit. If butchered by eight weeks of age, bucklings need not be castrated. If raised beyond that, they must be castrated to ensure good flavor and tender meat.

Mature older goats are butchered much like deer. Meat from yearlings is divided into the same cuts associated with lamb or beef. The meat of older animals is not as tender, so requires tenderizing with a marinade, or it may be ground into sausage and hamburger. Since goat is normally fat-free, it helps to add some pork fat or a tablespoon of vegetable oil to each pound of hamburger.

You may substitute goat meat for venison in any sausage recipe, or for beef if you add fat to compensate for lack of marbling. Making sausage requires a meat grinder and a sausage stuffer. Both come as optional attachments with the better household mixers such as Kitchenaid. There are books and catalogs on sausage making. Some are listed at the back of this book.

COMPOSITION OF GOAT MEAT AT VARIOUS AGES

	Birth	7 Weeks	22 Weeks	Yearling
Protein	78%	68%	59%	46%
Fat	8%	29%	36%	53%

From: Dairy Goat Management: Goats and the Tropics, 1984, International Dairy Goat Research Center, Prairie View, TX.

MEAT AS A PERCENTAGE OF LIVE WEIGHT*

	Birth	1.5 Months	5 Months	Yearling	Wether	Aged Doe
Pygmy	36%	47%	49%	52%	60%	45%
Other	21%	32%	34%	37%	45%	30%

*These are approximate percentages, varying with breed, condition, and the amount of digestive materials present at the time of weighing.

Goatkeepers who become attached to their animals may hire custom butchers or neighboring farmers to relieve themselves of emotional strain. Others prefer to sell meat animals through livestock auctions or ethnic meat markets to offset dairy costs. In some areas, buyers contact herders through local clubs or shows, and travel around during Easter and Passover to buy up surplus stock.

WETHERS FOR DRAFT

Since more bucklings than doelings are born every year, it seems a waste not to make good use of them. Many end up in the family freezer or are sold for meat, but there are other uses to which they can be put. Wethers aren't aggressive and have no odor. They make good pets, but, except for Pygmies, the market for pet wethers is very limited.

A wether may be used as a companion for a single doe where one milker is plenty, or as a playmate to keep a stud buck in shape. Some herders employ them as heat detectors, or to lead the herd when it forages over a large area during the day. Wethers will really earn their keep if trained for draft. And it's good exercise for them. Bucks, incidentally, can also be used for draft, provided they learn to respect their

A healthy herd of Pygmies are the playmates of this pint-size goatkeeper.
(Photo by Matto)

handler and do not get rough. Does lack the strength of bucks and wethers, and therefore are rarely used.

A draft wether may be harnessed to a row-crop cultivator or a small cart loaded to twice the animal's weight. Goat carts are fun for children, attract attention at parades and fairs, and are handy for hauling manure, bedding, firewood, hay, orchard fruit, and other light loads. Trained together, a two-wether team will pull double the load.

Start handling and training a draft wether early. When he is two months old, you should be able to lead him with a line. By six months, have him broken to a halter and understanding commands such as stop, go, left, and right. Use any command words you choose, as long as they sound different enough to avoid confusing the animal.

By eight months of age, the wether should be trained to accept a harness. By ten months, he should be ready to pull a light load, such as a board attached to the harness. Work patiently, talking to him and using his name often. Lead him around for half an hour twice daily, until he feels comfortable. Then add a heavier load, such as an old tire and rim. Whenever you change his load, let the animal smell and investigate it to calm his fears before he begins to pull.

By the time the goat is one year old, he should be ready to be hitched to an empty cart. Chances are he won't think much of the idea, so be gentle and patient. Every time he successfully executes a command, give him a treat. If you work with him just before feeding, he'll appreciate tidbits of his favorite foods as a reward, with his full ration at the end of the work session as something he will look forward to.

Once a goat is trained to pull a cart, it's easier to hitch him to a cultivator. But if you wish to use him only for garden work, begin training him to the cultivator when you would have hitched him to the empty cart.

Halters, harnesses, and goat carts may be purchased through dairy goat suppliers, or you can devise your own with an understanding of the purpose and function of each part. Cultivators are harder to find and require a diligent search.

A draft wether eats browse, grass hay, and a 9 percent protein ration. Take care he doesn't get fat. Keep him with a buddy, housing him in the dairy barn, with a stud buck or with a fellow wether for companionship.

(Photo by Matto)

Chapter 14

RUNNING
YOUR DAIRY
BUSINESS

Whether you keep goats for fun or for profit, it doesn't make much sense to spend needless time, effort, and money on them. But that's what will happen unless you decide from the outset to run your herd like a business.

This requires setting specific goals. Your goals might be to achieve a certain amount of milk, or a greater number of kids, per doe per year, or to improve milk quality, reduce kid losses, or minimize feed costs. If you're involved in commercial production, you'll strive for such things as selling a specific amount of milk each year, or increasing your market area at a certain steady rate. Review your goals at least once a year. If you're getting closer to some of them, set new ones or raise your standards so you'll always have something to reach for in the continuing process of improvement.

*Goat milk cheese being made at Le Chevier, Monroe, Tennessee.
(Photo by Matto)*

GOING COMMERCIAL

There are few really big goat dairies in this country, and some states have no commercial goat dairies. This creates a vast, untapped potential. But don't get the idea that just because your Aunt Tilly thinks goat milk is great, and your neighbors can't get enough of your homemade yogurt, that you're ready for the commercial world. Since the American consumer has not yet been educated to enjoy goat dairy products, a lot of market analysis must be done before you take that big step. If you can happily sell a little milk, yogurt, or cheese from your kitchen door, it might turn out that you're better off keeping it that way.

Identify Your Market

If you decide to become commercial, you'll need to make certain decisions so you won't founder around trying to get your business off the ground. Is there a market for goat milk in your area? How will you reach it? What will you sell, raw or pasteurized milk? Will you process dairy products? Will the sale of livestock provide a significant portion of your income? Will you learn A.I. techniques and do custom inseminating or semen collecting to augment your income?

Establishing your markets in advance and having more than one source of income will help you bring in a steady cash flow. Your ideas will doubtless change as you go along, but establishing a plan at the beginning will give you a clear path. Evaluate your plan periodically and make adjustments as required by changing market conditions and your own changing interests and needs.

Dairy Regulations

In some areas, you can engage in limited commercial sales without complying with any governmental regulations. In others, there are varying degrees of red tape that may include getting zoning approval or obtaining a permit. Where a license is needed, it pays to contact your state Extension dairy specialist and the dairy inspector from your state's Division of Food and Dairies at the onset. Both can make it easier for you to get governmental approval for your operation. Among the regulations you might encounter are meeting label specifications, allowing periodic inspection of your facilities, and providing milk samples to be analyzed for bacteria and antibiotics. In addition, certain building and equipment requirements must be met. Be well informed about these regulations to determine in advance whether you can afford the type of enterprise you have in mind.

Three Essentials

Regardless of its scope, a goat dairy requires the same three elements needed for most businesses—land, labor, and capital. If you don't own the land, tie down a long-term lease before you spend time and money developing facilities and markets. Be sure your location is suitable. If you can't handle all the work yourself, determine in advance whether other household members are willing to lend a hand or if you can find hired help at an affordable price. Your start-up costs may require minimal capital or a large reserve of funds, depending on existing facilities, the size and type of operation you have in mind, and the regulations you must comply with. Make sure you have access to enough capital to follow through with your plans until your dairy starts earning income.

COMMERCIAL DAIRY PRODUCTION	
Item	**Percentage of Total Cost**
Labor	41.1%
Feed	30.5%
Operating costs	15.5%
Return on investment (exclusive of processing plant)	7.0%
Replacement animals	3.8%
Depreciation (exclusive of processing plant)	3.3%
Sale of kids and culls	<1.2%>
Total	100%

Based on: G. F. W. Haenlein, "Dairy Goat Industry in the United States," *Journal of Dairy Sciences, 1981, 64:1288–1304.*

Creating a budget is essential to running a profitable goat dairy, whether for household use or commercial sales. Budgeting start-up costs will help you to determine if you have enough money for all the livestock, facilities, and supplies you need to get going. Once your herd is in full production, budgeting will tell you whether you're making or losing money.

To begin your budget, determine the total amount of milk and dairy products you can use or sell in one year. List them on a worksheet such as the accompanying one labeled "Returns." Then calculate the number of animals it would take to obtain the amount of milk you need. Fill in the meat and stock-sale columns based on these calculations.

Expenses

If you're like most household goatkeepers, you won't include labor on your "Expense" sheet. For home production, it is not necessary (nor necessarily desirable) to list labor, but for commercial dairies, it's essential. A commercial budget must include labor even if it's your own, since you're entitled to at least minimum wages. Besides, if you weren't herding goats, you'd presumably be doing some other profitable work. Other items not always listed in a home budget are interest and taxes. Interest should be included if you would have used your capital for an alternative money-making enterprise. Include property taxes if you purchase the land solely for business.

Once you have a projected budget on paper, look for ways to cut costs. Incorporate them into your goals. Perhaps you can develop a breeding plan that will keep your herd giving a steady supply of milk year-round. Or you can find cheaper alternative rations that will satisfy your herd's nutritional needs. You might target the lower quality, cheaper types of feeds for animals with lower nutritional needs, and save the more expensive, better quality rations for growing kids, pregnant does, and high-yield milkers. Study your budget and determine what your greatest expenses are to get other cost-cutting ideas.

Break-Even Point

Because of all the variables involved, it's impossible to specify a break-even point for dairy goats. Herders who have them solely for household use may pad the returns column with non-tangibles such as having access to better quality milk, the advantages of engaging in a family project, the exercise and fresh air obtained through herd management, or the entertainment value of shows and visiting other goatkeepers.

For commercial keepers, the break-even point can only be determined through cash income. For them, breaking even is most commonly measured in terms of milkers, since they produce most of the dairy income. Some experts quote 500 milkers as the break-even herd size. Others say 100 will do it. Some goatkeepers do well with fifty milkers, while others need only five. Why such a wide range?

Well, a five-milker dairy may break even, or possibly produce a positive cash flow, if all does efficiently convert feed into milk, if sales do not require complying with governmental regulations calling for expensive facilities and procedures, and if the reputation of the herd allows surplus kids to be sold at high prices. Some lucky off-farm sellers may break even at ten to fifteen milkers, but a Grade A dairy with all the necessary equipment must generate considerable income, which requires more milkers, which involves a greater distribution system, which in turn generates transportation and other associated expenses that may require additional milkers to further increase the income needed to break even.

It is therefore impossible to quote a single break-even figure applicable to every herd. Work out a budget based on your herd size, local values for milk and dairy products, and your costs for construction, rations, and supplies, to determine the break-even point for your situation. Even if you don't sell a single drop of milk, do your figuring based on the price you would have paid for milk and other dairy products enjoyed by your household. It's the only way to keep herd costs in line with the benefits. Obviously, the more efficiently your does produce, the fewer you will need, the lower your costs will be, and the easier it will be to break even.

KEEPING RECORDS

Along with budgeting, other records are essential to dairy herd management. But records are only as valuable as they are accurate. Don't try to keep them in your memory. Hang a calendar or pad in your milk parlor or other convenient place, and jot down things as they occur. In the evening, or at least once a week, transfer your notes to permanent record sheets where they will be neat and legible for easy reference.

Types of Records

Good records help you make important decisions about the future of your herd. They include breeder records to help you plan ahead for kidding, document breeding histories, arrange for a year-round milk supply, keep track of the individual breeding idiosyncrasies of your does, help detect normal and abnormal heat, and provide invaluable data for culling inefficient breeders.

BUDGET—EXPENSES

	UNIT	COST/UNIT	USEFUL LIFE	TOTAL
1. Animal Costs				
Does	2×	$125 ea.	÷ 5 yrs.	$ 50.00
Bucks	—		÷ 4	—
2. Housing Costs				
Land (fair rental)	2 acres	$10/ac./mo.	—	240.00
Shelter	140 sq. ft.	$18/sq. ft.	÷ 20	126.00
Fencing, yard	—		÷ 10	—
Fencing, pasture	1890 sq. ft.	55¢/sq. ft.	÷ 10	103.95
3. Equipment Costs				
Milking equipment	build milkstand	$ 35.00		7.00
	pails, etc.	$ 45.00	÷ 5	9.00
Milk processing equipment	cheese molds	$ 46.00		9.20
	separator	$395.00	÷ 5	79.00
Maintenance equipment	castrator	$ 25.00		5.00
	disbudding	$ 30.00	÷ 5	6.00
4. Maintenance Costs				
Bedding (straw)	5 bales	1.25/bale	÷ 1 yr.	6.25
Hay	50 bales	1.25/bale	1	62.50
Concentrate	2250 lb.	$12.00/cwt.	1	270.00
Medications & Veterinarian			1	25.00
Breeding fees	3	10 ea.	1	30.00
Repairs & Supplies			1	30.00
Water & Electricity			1	—
Pasture upkeep	seed, fertilizer, tractor use		1	146.00
Labor			1	—
Insurance			1	—
5. Capital Costs				
Interest on 1+2+3	$635.15	@10%	1	63.52
Property taxes			1	
GRAND TOTAL			1 yr.	$1,268.42

BUDGET—EXPENSES

	UNIT	COST/UNIT	USEFUL LIFE	TOTAL
1. Animal Costs				
Does				
Bucks				
2. Housing Costs				
Land (fair rental)				
Shelter				
Fencing, yard				
Fencing, pasture				
3. Equipment Costs				
Milking equipment				
Milk processing equipment				
Maintenance equipment				
4. Maintenance Costs				
Bedding (straw)				
Hay				
Concentrate				
Medications & Veterinarian				
Breeding fees				
Repairs & Supplies				
Water & Electricity				
Pasture upkeep				
Labor				
Insurance				
5. Capital Costs				
Interest on 1 + 2 + 3				
Property taxes				
GRAND TOTAL				

Health care records include when and how often your goats are vaccinated and wormed, as well as problems with mastitis and other health conditions. These records will indicate the need for more careful preventive management, or the necessity to cull weak and susceptible animals from your herd.

Ration records that include how much feed you use, and what kind, help you trace nutrition-related problems. If you also keep detailed records on what you pay for each type of feed, you will be better able to find ways to cut costs.

All income and expenses should be well documented so you can keep track of profits and losses, analyze proposed changes, and make informed decisions about your alternatives. If yours is a commercial dairy, complete records are necessary for filing income tax returns, and may help you obtain credit by demonstrating your potential for future income.

Additional records include periodically updated inventories. A capital inventory lists assets—including livestock, facilities, and equipment—to show you where you've been, where you stand, and where you're headed. A supplies inventory tells you what items are getting low and must be ordered. By referring back to past supply inventories, you may discover things you use up faster than you anticipated, for which purchase in bulk quantities may be cheaper.

Home Computers

An excellent way to keep records is on a home computer. Computers allow concise and accurate record-keeping, help you make predictions based on the past, and eliminate the emotional aspect when analyzing management decisions. As of this writing there is no commercially available software designed specifically for goat dairies, but there are many programs for dairy management, ration formulation, farm finances, and breeding. They are more or less adaptable to dairy goats, depending on the specific software design and your own computer skills. You might even design your own software based on your particular needs. If you go on test, you can tie in with the DHIA on-line computer service for ready reference to your herd's records.

Whether you keep a herd for household use, recreation, or to turn a profit, comprehensive and accurate records play an important role in raising milk goats successfully.

BUDGET—RETURNS

		COST/UNIT	UNITS/YEAR	TOTAL
Returns				
Milk		$2.19/gal.	195 gal.	$ 427.05
Dairy products	yogurt	2.05/qt.	146 qt.	299.30
	hard cheese	3.30/lb.	52 lb.	171.60
	cottage cheese	2.25/lb.	12 lb.	27.00
	butter	2.25/lb.	84 lb.	189.00
Meat				
Stock	milker	$125/doe	1 per yr.	125.00
	doelings	$ 35/kid	1 per yr.	35.00
	bucklings	$ 18/kid	2 per yr.	36.00
GRAND TOTAL				$1,309.95

This example is based on an actual small family herd. A larger herd is more efficient since some of the costs do not grow in proportion to herd size.

BUDGET—RETURNS

		COST/UNIT	UNITS/YEAR	TOTAL
Returns				
Milk		_____	_____	_____
Dairy products	yogurt	_____	_____	_____
	hard cheese	_____	_____	_____
	cottage cheese	_____	_____	_____
	butter	_____	_____	_____
Meat		_____	_____	_____
Stock	milker	_____	_____	_____
	doelings	_____	_____	_____
	bucklings	_____	_____	_____
GRAND TOTAL		_____	_____	_____

Appendix A

BOOKS, SUPPLIES, SERVICES

REFERENCE BOOKS

Artificial Insemination

Artificial Insemination and Genetic Improvement of Dairy Goats, by Dr. Harry A. Herman, 28 Fleming Drive, Columbia, MO 65201. Covers collecting, processing, storing, and shipping semen; A.I. techniques for improving milk production, conformation, and economic value.

Artificial Insemination Handbook, Vaughn Solomon and Donna Forsman. Magnum Semen Works, 2200 Albert Hill Road, Hampstead, MD 21074. Introduction to dairy goat A.I. by former owners of Magnum Semen Works.

Artificial Insemination of Diary Goats. American Dairy Goat Association, Box 865, Spindale, NC 28160. Pamphlet covering the basics.

Breed Books

The Illustrated Standard of the Dairy Goat—a Guide for Evaluating and Judging Conformation, Nancy Lee Owen. Caprine Supply, Box Y, DeSoto, KS 66218. Illustrated guide to the ideal goat in each of the main dairy breeds; guidelines for buying, breeding, culling, showing, and milking.

Nubian History: American & Great Britain, Alice Hall. Hall Press, Box 52750, San Bernardino, CA 92412. Originally written in 1947 by Mrs. Robert Reinhart, updated and revised by Hall in 1978.

The Pygmy in America, Alice Hall. Hall Press, Box 5375. San Bernardino, CA 92412. Lots of good tips on general management and showing but lacking in details specific to Pygmies.

Saanen Roots, Allan L. Rogers. Caprine Supply, Box Y, DeSoto, KS 66218. Detailed history of Saanens.

Cheesemaking

Cheesemaking Made Easy, Ricki and Robert Carroll. Storey Communications, Inc., Schoolhouse Road, Pownal, VT 05261. Recipes for 60 kinds of soft and hard cheese, some specifically from goat milk.

The Fabrication of Farmstead Goat Cheese, Jean-Claude Le Jaouen, American Cheese Society, 157 West 93rd Street, New York, NY 10025. Recipes for over 70 kinds of goat cheese, plans for building a cheese room; considered the cheesemakers bible.

Goat Cheese Small Scale Production, Mont-Laurier Benedictine Nuns. New England Cheesemaking Supply Company, Box 85, Ashfield, MA 01330. Recipes for cheese, butter, and yogurt by the Benedictine Nuns of Mont Laurier, Canada.

Facilities

Building Small Barns, Sheds & Shelters, Monte Burch. Storey Communications, Inc., Schoolhouse Road, Pownal, VT 05261. Confidence-building basic skills and a variety of specific plans.

Practical Pole Building Construction, Leigh Seddon. Williamson Publishing Company, Church Hill Road, Box 185, Charlotte, VT 05445. Plans for quick and easy, low-cost barns for readers with basic construction know-how.

Smooth-Wire Tension Fencing—Design and Construction, Mark Mummert, et al. The Pennsylvania State University, College of Agriculture, Cooperative Extension Service, University Park, PA 16802. Pamphlet covering basic design and construction of New Zealand style fencing.

Health Care

Fundamentals of Improved Dairy Goat Management, R. A. Jackson, DVM, and Alice Hall. Hall Press, Box 5375, San Bernardino, CA 92412, 714-887-3466. Herd health handbook co-authored to combine the experience of a goatkeeper with the knowledge of a veterinarian.

Goat Health Handbook, Winrock International Livestock Research Training Center, Petit Jean Mountain, Morrilton, AK 72110, 501-727-5435. Excellent manual on diagnosis and therapy for bacterial, viral, metabolic and parasitic diseases.

The Goatkeeper's Veterinary Book, Peter Dunn, B.V.Sc., Farming Press Ltd., Wharfedale Road, Ipswich, Suffolk, England. Prevention and treatment of over 150 ailments from a British perspective.

Management and Diseases of Dairy Goats, Sam B. Guss, DVM. Caprine Supply, Box Y, DeSoto, KS 66218. Authoritative but somewhat dated guide to nutrition, housing, parasites, reproduction, and surgery.

Management

Dairy Goats: Breeding/Feeding/Management, Byrin E. Colby, et. al. American Dairy Goat Association, Box 865, Spindale, NC 28160. Excellent introduction to management.

USDA Goat Extension Handbook, George Haenlein and Donald L. Ace, editors. National Dairy Herd Improvement Association, 3021 E. Dublin-Granville Road, Columbus, OH 43229. Sixty informative articles in a three-ring binder.

Goat Husbandry, David MacKenzie. Faber and Faber, 50 Cross Street, Winchester, MA 01890. British book written in 1957 and revised by Jean Laing in 1980; a collection of theories, scientific facts and personal experiences widely considered the goatkeepers' Bible.

Raising Goats for Milk and Meat, Rosalee Sinn, Heifer Project International, Box 808, Little Rock, AR 72203. Spiral-bound beginner's manual, perfect for 4-H.

Additional publications may be available free from your state Agricultural Extension office. Some treat goats as miniature cows, some use technical terms without defining them, but most contain helpful information—and the price is right.

Meat Processing

Butchering, Processing, and Preservation of Meat, Frank G. Ashbrook. Van Nostrand Reinhold Company, 135 West 50th Street, New York, NY 10020. Good all-around reference but with no specific details on goats—follow directions for sheep or deer; includes curing, canning, and sausage making.

Chevon Recipes, Caprine Supply, Box Y, DeSoto, KS 66218. Nicely illustrated booklet with over 70 recipes from backyard barbecue to exotic foreign fair.

Great Sausage Recipes and Meat Curing, Rytek Kutas. The Sausagemaker, 177 Military Road, Buffalo, NY 14207. Definitive work with over 175 recipes by a professional sausagemaker; nothing specifically on goat meat—follow directions for any lean meat.

Nutrition

The following two books are available at many libraries. Both are fairly technical.

Feeds and Nutrition, M. E. Ensminger and C. G. Olentine, Jr. Ensminger Publishing Company, 3699 Sierra Avenue, Clovis, CA 93612. Internationally used guide to the fundamentals of livestock nutrition; abridged version is less technical and less expensive; chapter 22 covers goats.

Nutrient Requirements of Goats, National Research Council, National Academy Press, 2101 Constitution Avenue, Washington, DC 20418. Ninety-one pages of text, tables, and bibliographic references compiled from direct studies (not derived from research on cattle or sheep).

PERIODICALS

Dairy Goat Journal, 6041 Monona Drive, Monona, WI 53716, 608-222-1108, 800-272-4628. Monthly magazine.

Footnotes*, 209 Crown Road, Willow Park, TX 76087. Quarterly magazine on Nigerian Dwarfs.

Goat Notes & News, RR 6, Bloomfield, IA 52537. Monthly newsletter covering all breeds.

United Caprine News, PO Drawer A, Rotan, TX 78546, 915-735-2278. Monthly newspaper covering all breeds.

CORRESPONDENCE COURSES

Dairy Goat Production, #225, Independent Study, University of Guelph, Guelph, Ontario, Canada NIG 2WI. Lessons include housing, breeding, feeding, kidding, and herd health. Suitable for individual study or group training. Includes 93 slides on a filmstrip adaptable to a slide projector, and two audio tapes.

Dairy Goats, The Pennsylvania State University, 307 Agricultural Administration Building, University Park, PA 16802. Nine lessons on dairy goat origins, characteristics, breeding, feeding, care and management, equipment and housing. Includes availability of experts to answer your questions.

RESEARCH FACILITIES

The following research facilities sponsor courses, demonstrations, tours, and dairy goat field days. All publish up-to-the-minute research findings in an easy-to-read style.

E. "Kiki" de la Garza Institute for Goat Research, Box 730, Langston, OK 73050, 405-466-3836. Geared primarily toward Oklahoma; will add your name to mailing list on request.

Dairy Goat Research Facility, University of California at Davis, Animal Science Department, Davis, CA 95616, 916-752-1250. Subscription to quarterly newsletter available from: A.N.R. Publications, University of California, 6701 San Pablo Avenue, Oakland, CA 94608.

International Dairy Goat Research Center, College of Agriculture, Drawer U, Prairie View A & M University, Prairie View, TX 77446, 409-857-3926. Will add your name to mailing list on request.

ORGANIZATIONS

Most of the following organizations are run by volunteers so their addresses change periodically. For current addresses and listings of additional regional and local clubs, consult *Dairy Goat Journal, United Caprine News,* or the American Dairy Goat Association.

Alpines International, Joan B. Godfrey, Secretary, 557 South Street, Suffield, CT 06078.

American Cheese Society, c/o Anna Herman, 157 West 93rd Street, New York, NY 10025, 212-932-1018. Annual convention and cheese judging competition, bi-monthly newsletter.

American Dairy Goat Association, Box 865, Spindale, NC 28160, 704-286-3801. Largest registry for the six main dairy breeds; publishes directory and numerous informative booklets.

American Goat Society, Wayne Hamrick, Secretary, Route 2, Box 112, DeLeon, TX 76444. Registers six main dairy breeds as well as Pygmies, Nigerian Dwarves (a small breed similar to Pygmies), and Sable Saanens; quarterly newsletter.

American LaMancha Association, Gerri Horka, Secretary, 103-156th Place, Calumet City, IL 60409.

Canadian Goat Society, Box 357, Fergus, Ontario, Canada N1M 3E2.

International Dairy Goat Registry, Route 1 Box 265-A, Rossville, GA 30741. Registers all breeds; on-site library and archive.

International Nubian Breeders Association, Shirley Gardner, Secretary, Box 130, Creswell, OR 97426.

National Pygmy Goat Association, Nancy Brewer, Secretary, 5113 Smyrna Road, Richmond, IN 47374.

National Saanen Breeders Association, Mimi Waterman, 33 Kerr Road, Canterbury, CT 06331.

National Toggenburg Club, Janice McMahon, Secretary, Box 531, Fort Collins, CO 80522.

Nigerian Dwarf Goat Foundation, Cathy Claps, Secretary, Route 1 Box 368, Red Rock, TX 78662.

Oberhasli Breeders of America, JoAnn Clugston, 2214 Mountain Road, Manheim, PA 17545.

Sable Breeders Association, Suzy Wiese, Secretary, Box 384, Mead, WA 99021.

SUPPLIES

The following sources are offered, with no endorsement implied, to give you a start in locating specialized dairy goat supplies and services.

Artificial Insemination

Buck Bank, 2344 Butte Falls Highway, Eagle Point, OR 97524, 503-826-2729. Supplies, semen, custom collection, video.

HBF Caprine Services, Thurman and Jane Jaggers, Route 1 Box 110, Buffalo Valley, TN 38548, 615-858-2482. Supplies, semen, custom collection, courses.

Kentucky Caprine Services, Route 6 Box 2, Leithfield, KY 42754, 502-242-7079. Supplies, semen custom collection, courses, embryo transfer.

Magnum Semen Works, Wayne and Carol Rhoten, 2200 Albert Hill Road, Hampstead, MD 21074, 301-374-2927. Supplies semen, custom collection, one-day classes.

Cheesemaking

New England Cheesemaking Supply Company, Box 85, Ashfield, MA 01330, 413-628-3808.

The Cheesemaking Supply Outlet, RD 3 Walheim Road, Parker, PA 16049, 412-791-2449.

Butchering

Norseman Sausage Supplies, Route 2 Box 141-A, Wellsville, KS 66092. Sausagemaking and cured-meat supplies.

Pioneer, 1725 Dotsero Ave, Loveland, CO 80537, 303-669-1094. Home butcher supplies and equipment.

The Sausagemaker, 177 Military Road, Buffalo, NY 14207. Complete line of equipment and supplies to make sausage and cured-meat products.

Hutches (Portable Housing)

L. T. Hampel Corp, Box 39, Germantown, WI 53022, 414-255-4540, 800-558-8558. Polyethylene hutches with lifetime guarantee.

Pet Castle Company, POB 1059, Brownwood, TX 76801, 915-643-2517, 800-381-1363. Molded plastic huts for kids.

Poly Dome Inc., RR 1 Box 13, Litchfield, MN 55355, 612-693-8370, 800-328-7659. Variety of large and small hutches, three-year guarantee.

VIC, 111 Maple Drive, Spring Grove, MN 55974, 507-498-5577, 800-537-7145. Fiberglass hutches in two sizes, lifetime warranty.

Management

American Supply House, Box 1114, Columbia, MO 65205, 314-449-6264. Supplies, books.

Caprine Supply, Box Y, DeSoto, KS 66018, 913-585-1191. Supplies, books; catalog crammed with goatkeeping tips.

Harvey Considine, W10802 Walker Road, Portage, WI 53901, 608-742-6554. Professional herd evaluation service.

Hoegger Supply Company, Box 331, Fayetteville, GA 30214, 404-461-4129. Equipment, supplies, books.

Nasco Farm and Ranch, 901 Janesville Avenue, Ft. Atkinson, WI 52538, 414-563-2446, 800-558-9595. Dairy, A.I. and general equipment, books.

Spalding Laboratories, 760 Printz Road, Arroyo Grande, CA 93420, 805-489-5946. Beneficial insects for fly control.

Milking Equipment

Canadian Home Dairy Supply Company, RR 8, Moncton, R1V 8K2, Canada, 506-384-8803.

Michael Lawyer, Box 326, Neoga, IL 62447, 217-895-3906. Reconditioned portable milking machines.

Pro Goat Products, RD #1 Box 193, Richfield Springs, NY 13439, 315-866-7680. Portable milking machines.

W. P. Lang, RR #1 Box 394, Evanston, IN 47531, 812-529-8371. Portable milk stands.

Pete Humphreys, Thurstaston Acres, 11302 East Hash Knife Circle, Tucson, AZ 85749, 602-749-4543. Milk stand construction plans.

Nutritional Supplements

Alpine Cottage, 59520 Springdale Drive, Hartford, MI 49057. Herbal supplements, books.

Dairy Goat Nutrition, Box 22363, Kansas City, MO 64113, 816-361-3020, 800-445-0623. Vitamins, minerals, colostrum, milk replacers.

Nutritional Research Associates, Box 354, South Whitley, IN 46787, 219-723-4931. Minerals, supplements, medications, books.

Vita Stress, 24024 Bollenbough Hill Road, Monroe, WA 98272, 206-794-9663. Vitamin/protein/mineral supplement.

Fences

Kencove Fence, 111 Kendall Lane, Blairsville, PA 15717, 412-459-8991, 800-245-6902. High tensile fences and supplies.

Premier, Box 89, Washington, IA 52353, 319-653-6631. Permanent and portable fences and supplies; the only American film researching confinement of goats.

Multi-Tech, Box A, Marlboro, NJ 07746, 201-431-0550, 800-431-3223. High tensile fences and supplies.

New Zealand Fence Systems, Box 518, Boring, OR 97009, 503-658-6565, 800-222-6849. High tensile fences and supplies.

Waterford Corporation, Box 1513, Fort Collins, CO 80522, 303-482-0911, 800-525-4952. Permanent and portable fences and supplies.

West Virginia Fence Corporation, US Route 219, Lindside, WV 24951, 304-753-4387, 800-356-5458. Permanent and portable fences and supplies.

Software

Pedigree Plus, Marigold Company, 725 Trout Gulch Road, Aptos, CA 95003, 408-662-0987. Pedigree and show software for Macintosh.

St. Benedict's Farm, Box 366, Waelder, TX 78959, 512-540-4814. Pedigree and record-keeping software for IBM-PC compatibles.

The Key Board, Box 753, Cedar Crest, NM 87008, 505-281-1795. Show software for IBM-PC compatibles.

Visual Aids

Some of the following visual aids may be rented, some may be borrowed through state Extension offices, some must be purchased outright.

Vocational Education Products, California Polytechnic State University, San Luis Obispo, CA 93407, 805-756-2295 (slides).

Instructional Media Center, Marketing Division, Michigan State University, Box 710, East Lansing, MI 48826, 517-353-9229 (slides, videos).

John C. Porter, Extension Dairy Specialist, Dairy, Merrimack County Office, 327 Daniel Webster Highway, Boscawen, NH 03303, 603-225-5505 (slides).

University of California at Davis, Visual Media Department, Davis, CA 95616 (slides, films, videos).

Winrock International, Technical and Informational Services, Route 3, Morrilton, AR 72110 (slides).

Veterinary

Jeffers Vet Supply, Box 100, Dothan, AL 36302, 205-793-6257, 800-633-7592.

Northern Wholesale Veterinary Supply, N5570 Frontage Road, Highway 53, North Onalaska, WI 54650, 608-783-0300, 800-356-5852.

Omaha Vaccine Company, Box 7228, Omaha, NE 68107, 402-731-1155.

PBS Livestock Drugs, Box 9101, Canton, OH 44711, 800-321-0235, 800-362-9838.

Appendix B

GOATKEEPERS' JARGON

Abomasum. The fourth, and second largest, chamber of a ruminant's stomach, where actual digestion takes place.

Acidosis. Condition in which rumen pH falls, usually because the goat ate too much grain or lush forage.

A.I. Artificial Insemination; also, Alpines International.

American. A dairy goat with verifiable ancestry that's at least $\frac{7}{8}$ purebred for a doe and $\frac{15}{16}$ for a buck.

Anestrus. Time during which a doe does not experience heat cycles.

*B. Star Buck; recognition based on production records of the buck's ancestry.

+B. Plus buck; recognition based on production records of the buck's progeny.

Barrel. Entire body cavity; also, the girth of the body cavity at its largest circumference near the last rib.

Blind Teat. One that is non-functional because of defect, injury, or disease.

Bloat. Gastritis; accumulation of gas in the rumen.

Bolus. Large, oval pill; also, the cud.

Breeding Apron. Device used on a buck to prevent mating.

Buck Rag. Cloth rubbed on the scent glands of a buck and used to induce or detect heat in does.

Butterfat. Cream.

Cabrito. Literally, "little goat," Spanish designation used in the Southwest for kid meat.

CAE. Caprine Arthritis Encephalitis, a prevalent disease easily prevented by heat-treating all colostrum and milk fed to kids.

California Mastitis Test. Home method of testing milk to determine if a doe has mastitis.

Caprine. Of or pertaining to goats.

Caproic Acid. A fatty acid that makes raw goat milk taste "goaty" with age.

Carotene. A compound that becomes vitamin A after ingestion.

Chevon. French designation for goat meat used in the East.

Chèvre. Classic French soft cheese made from goat milk.

Classification. Score given a goat based on appearance.

Closed Herd Book. Record of registration of goats resulting from the mating of dam and sire already registered in the closed herd book.

CMT. California Mastitis Test.

Colostrum. Thick, yellow first milk a doe gives after kidding, high in protein, vitamins, and antibodies to protect her kids from infection.

Corpus Luteum. Yellow body; solid yellowish mass of tissue that develops in a doe's ovary after an egg has been released.

Cryptorchidism. Undescended testicle(s).

Cud. Soft mass of food regurgitated and rechewed by a ruminant.

Curd. Coagulated milk.

Dam. Female parent.

DHIA. Dairy Herd Improvement Association, administered by the USDA.

DHIR. Dairy Herd Improvement Registry, production testing program administered by dairy goat registries in cooperation with the DHIA.

Disbud. To remove the horn cells of a young goat.

Dished. Slightly concave facial profile characteristic of Pygmies and some of the Swiss breeds.

Drench. A liquid medication; also, to administer a liquid medication.

Dry Doe. Mature doe that is not lactating.

Dry Off. To stop giving milk at the end of a lactation period.

Elf Ear. LaMancha ear up to two inches long.

Enterotoxemia. Toxic indigestion that may follow acidosis.

Estrous Cycle. A series of seventeen to twenty-three day cycles during which a doe comes into regular periodic heat.

Estrus. Heat; periodic sexual excitement during which a doe permits mating.

Flush. To increase a doe's nutritional supply of energy and thereby stimulate ovulation and conception.

Foot Rot. Fungus infection causing lameness.

Free Choice. Method of feeding in which rations are always present.

Freshen. To begin lactation after giving birth.

Gopher Ear. LaMancha ear one inch long or less with no cartilage.

Grade. A doe having one parent registered as a purebred and the other of mixed or unknown ancestry.

Grading Up. The process of breeding successive generations of grade does to purebred bucks until they qualify as American for their breed.

Heart Girth. Circumference of the chest just behind the front legs.

Heat. Sexual readiness; estrus.

Herd. More than one goat.

Hermaphrodite. An animal with both male and female sex organs.

In Kid. Pregnant.

Intersex. Neither wholly male nor wholly female.

Lactating. Giving milk.

Legume. Group of plants that includes alfalfa and clover.

Let Down. Release of milk by the mammary gland.

*M. Star milker; recognition on the basis of superior milking abilities; number of stars designates the number of superior milkers in the doe's immediate ancestry.

Mange. Contagious, itchy skin disease caused by mites.

Manger. A trough that holds feed.

Mastitis. Inflammatory disease of the udder.

Mites. Tiny parasites that feed on skin and blood.

Off Feed. Not eating as much as usual.

Omasum. One of the compartments of a ruminant's stomach, also called many ply.

On Test. Enrolled in the DHIA milk testing program.

Papers. Certificates of recordation or registration.

Parlor. Place where does are milked.

Placenta. Afterbirth.

Progeny. Offspring.

Recordation. Documentation of a crossbred or a grade dairy goat on record with a registry.

Registration. Documentation of a purebred or American goat on record with a registry.

Reticulum. Second of the four chambers of a ruminant's stomach.

Ringworm. Contagious fungal disease.

Roman. Convex facial profile characteristic of Nubians.

Rumen. First and largest of the four chambers of a ruminant's stomach.

Ruminant. An animal with a four-chambered stomach that chews its cud.

Scours. Severe diarrhea.

Scrotum. Hanging pouch containing a buck's testicles.

Scrub. A goat of unknown ancestry.

Scur. Odd-shaped horn resulting from improper disbudding.

Settle. Get pregnant; conceive.

Shipping Fever. Pneumonia accompanied by diarrhea, usually resulting from travel stress.

Silent Heat. In heat but showing no outward signs.

Sire. Male parent.

Stanchion. A restraining device that holds a goat by the neck.

Standing Heat. Doe's receptivity to being mated.

Unrecorded Grade. A doe whose ancestry is either unknown or just not recorded.

Uterus. Womb.

Index

A
Abomasum, 32, 33, 165
Abortion, 79–80
Abscesses, 127–128
Acidosis, 129, 165
Acini, 114
Afterbirth, 85
Age, 18
Alpine breed, 9, 10
Alveoli, 114
American, 165
Anestrus, 165
Arthritis, 99, 131
Artificial insemination, 77–78

B
Barrel, 165
Birth chilling, 99
Black scours, 99
Blind teat, 165
Bloat, 128–129, 165
Bloody scours, 99
Boils, 127–128
Bolus, 165
Bones, broken, 131
Break-even point, 151–152
Breeds, 8–15
  comparison, 14
Breeders
  choosing, 65–74
  evaluating, 69
Breeding, 75–86
  failure to conceive, 78–79
  time for, 76
Breeding apron, 165
Broken bones, 161
Browse, 37–38
Buck rag, 165
Bucks
  de-scenting, 64
  housing, 30
  infertility, 128
  problems, 128
  rations, 42
  selection, 18–19
Budgeting, 151–152, 153–154, 156
Butter, 109

C
Cabrito, 165
CAE. See Caprine Arthritis Encephalitis
  (CAE)
Calcium, 47
California Mastitis Test (CMT), 166

Caprine Arthritis Encephalitis (CAE), 131,
  134, 165
Caproic acid, 105, 166
Carbohydrates, 44
Castrating, 96
Cheese, 110–112
Chlorine, 49
Cleanliness, 55–56
Clipping wattles, 93
Closed herd book, 166
Coccidiosis, 99, 128
Colibacillosis, 99
Colostrum, 87, 89, 166
Computers, 155
Concentrates, 40–41
  nutritional composition, 44
  protein content, 51
Conception, factors influencing, 82–83
Conditioning, 139
Constipation, 98
Contagious ecthymia, 132
Corpus luteum, 166
Cream, 109
Crossbreeding, 67
Cryptorchidism, 166

D
Dairy
  business, 147–156
    break-even point, 151–152
    budgeting, 151–152, 153–154, 156
    expenses, 153–154
    market identification, 149
    record keeping, 152–155
  character of a goat, 16, 17
  goat management, 53–64
    seasonal reminders, 63
  regulations, 149
Dairy Herd Improvement (DHI) testing,
  107
Dairy Herd Improvement Association,
  107, 166
Dairy Herd Improvement Registry (DHIR),
  107–108, 166
Dams, choosing, 65–74
De-scenting, 64, 95, 97
Dehorning, 61–62
Demodex mange, 134
Diarrhea, 98, 99, 128
Dietary deficiencies, clinical signs of, 48
Digestive upset, 128–129
Disbudding, 62, 94–95, 97, 166
Diseases of kids, 99
Does, handling, 104

Draft wethers, 144–145
Drench, 166
Drying off, 117–119, 166

E
E. coli Septicemia, 99
Ears, 129
Electrolyte formula, 98
Energy, 44–45
Enterotoxemia, 129, 166
Estrous cycle, 167
Estrus, 71–74, 167. *See also* Heat
   manipulating, 71–72
Exercise, 28, 30
Expenses, 151, 153–154
External parasites, 134–135
Eyes, 129

F
Fats, 44
Feed. *See* Rations
Feed storage, 25
Feeding kids, 89–92
Feeding practices, 33
Fences, 28–29
Fertility, factors influencing, 82–83
Fertilizer, 142
Flushing, 75–76, 167
Foot rot, 131, 167
Forage, 37–40
   rotation, 39–40
Freezing, 130
Freshening, 117, 167
Fuerstenberg's rosette, 114

G
Gas, 128–129
Gates, 28–29
Genital hypoplasia, 79
Gestation, 80–81. *See also* Kidding
Gland cistern, 114
Goats. *See also* Bucks; Does; Kids
   breeds, 8–15
   choosing, 15
   examining, 16
   grade, 15, 167
   handling, 55
   normal vital statistics, 122
   transporting, 55
   weighing, 59–60
   weight, estimating, 60
   where to buy, 19–20
Grade, 15, 167
Grain storage, 25
Grazing, 38
Grooming, 56–57

H
Hair styles, 57
Handling
   does, 104
   goats, 55
   kids, 97
   milk, 105–106

Hay, 34–37
   needs, 34–35
   pelleted, 37
   quality evaluation, 36
   sources, 37
   storage, 25, 37
Health
   care, 121–126, 121
   care records, 155
   checks, 122
   kids, 98–99
   maintenance, 126
Heat, 71–74, 167
   abnormal, 73
   factors influencing, 82–83
   recognizing, 72–74
Herd book, closed, 166
Herd disposal sales, 19
Heritability of certain traits, 68
Hermaphroditism, 79, 167
Hoof rot. *See* Foot rot
Hoof trimming, 58–59
Housing, 21–30
   bucks, 30
   cleaning, 56
   plan, 22
   requirements, 29
Hypoglycemia, 99

I
Inbreeding, 66
Indigestion, 128–129
Infertility in bucks, 128
Injections, 125–126
Internal parasites, 136
Intersex, 79, 167
Iodine, 49

J
Joint swelling, 131

K
Keyhole mangers, 23–24
Kidding, 84–85, 87
   abnormal, 86
Kids
   care, 87–101
   diseases, 99
   feeding, 89–92
   feeding schedule, 90
   general care, 96–97
   handling, 97
   health, 98–99
   starter ration, 92
   stomach development, 33
   training, 97

L
LaMancha breed, 8, 9, 10
Lameness, 131
Let down, 167
Linebreeding, 67
Livestock auction, 19
Lobes, 114

Lobules, 114

M
Magnesium, 47–49
Maiden milker, 117
Mange, 134, 167
Mangers, 23–24
Mastitis, 115–117, 167
Meat, 142–144
  as percentage of live weight, 143
  composition of, 143
Medications
  injections, 125–126
  oral, 124
Milk, 101–112
  canals, 114
  handling, 105–106
  how to, 103
  off-flavored, 106
  parlor, 25–27
  replacer, 91
  solids, average, 102
  stand, 26–28
Milking
  equipment, 104–105
  procedure, 102–104
  records, 17
Minerals, 47–50
Mites, 129, 134, 167
Mouth sores, 132
Myoepithelial cells, 114

N
Navel ill, 99
Nubian breed, 8, 9, 11
Nutrients, essential, 44–45
Nutrition, 43–51

O
Oberhasli breed, 8, 9, 11
Omasum, 32, 33, 168
Omphalitis, 99
On test, 107–108, 168
Oral medications, 124
Outbreeding, 67

P
Parasites
  external, 134–135
  internal, 136
Pasteurization, 105–106
Pasture, 38–39
Phosphorus, 47
Pinkeye, 129
Placenta, 85
Pneumonia, 99, 133–134
Poisoning, 132–133
Post-kidding doe care, 85
Potassium, 49
Pregnancy, 80–81. See also Kidding
Private sales, 20
Progeny testing, 69

Protein, 45
  balancing, 40
  content of sample concentrates, 51
Purebreds, 15
Pygmy breed, 8, 9, 12

R
Rations, 31–42
  balancing, 43–44
  records, 155
  starter, 92
Recordation, 168
Records
  keeping, 152-155
  milking, 17
Registration, 168
Respiratory problems, 133–134
Reticulum, 32, 33, 168
Ringworm, 134, 168
Roughage, 34–37
Rumen, 32, 33, 168
  function, 34
Ruminants, 33–34, 168

S
Saanen breed, 8, 12, 13
Salmonellosis, 99
Sarcoptic mange, 134
Scours, 98, 99, 168
  black, 99
  bloody, 99
Selective breeding, 65–68
Selenium, 50
Shipping fever, 168
Showing, 137–141
  conditioning, 139
  training, 139
  typical judges' scorecard, 140
Sires, choosing, 65–74
Skin conditions, 134–135
Sodium, 49
Sodium bicarbonate, 49
Soremouth, 132
Starter ration, kids, 92
Stomach, 32, 33
Streak canal, 114
Stress, 19–20
  avoiding, 54
Sulfur, 49
Sunburn, 134
Sunflower seeds, 37

T
Tattoo year code, 93
Tattooing, 93
Teat cistern, 114
Temperature, 123–124
Testing, 107–108
Toggenburg breed, 8, 13
Training, 139
  kids, 97
Transporting goats, 55
Trouble shooting, 127–136

U

Udder
care, 113–120
cistern, 114
components, 113–115
dry period treatment, 120
evaluation, 119
examining, 17
injury, 115

V

Virgin milker, 117
Vitamins, 45–46

W

Water, 50–51
Waterers, 25
Wattles, clipping, 93
Weaning, 92
Weighing, 59–60
Weight, estimating, 60
Wethers, draft, 144–145
Worms, 136
Wounds, 134

Y

Yard, 28
Yogurt, 109

WILLIAMSON PUBLISHING CO.

BOX 185, CHURCH HILL ROAD,
CHARLOTTE, VERMONT 05445

More Good Books from

☀ WILLIAMSON PUBLISHING

PRACTICAL POLE BUILDING CONSTRUCTION
by Leigh Seddon

Saves money, time, labor; no excavation. Complete how-to-build information with *original* architectural plans and specs for small barn, horse barn, shed, animal shelter, cabins and more.

176 pages, 8½×11, over 100 architectural renderings, tables, charts. Quality paperback, $9.95.

BUILDING FENCES FROM WOOD, STONE, METAL, AND LIVING PLANTS
by John Vivian

Complete how-to on wood fence, stone fence, block, brick & mud fence, living fence & hedgerow, primitive fence, wire livestock fence, electric barrier fence, and classic horse fence.

192 pages, 8½×11, hundreds of drawings & photos, tables, charts. Quality paperback, $12.95.

THE SHEEP RAISER'S MANUAL
by William Kruesi

"Don't raise sheep without it." **The New Farm**

"Overall, *The Sheep Raiser's Manual* does a better job of integrating all aspects of sheep farming into a successful sheep enterprise than any other book published in the United States." **Dr. Paul Saenger New England Farmer**

280 pages, 6×9, illustrations, photos, charts & tables. Quality paperback, $13.95.

RAISING PIGS SUCCESSFULLY
by Kathy and Bob Kellogg

Everything you need to know for the perfect low-cost, low-work pig raising operation. Choosing piglets, to housing, feeds, care, breeding, slaughtering, packaging, and even cooking your home grown pork.

224 pages, 6×9, illustrations, photos, tables. Quality paperback, $8.95.

RAISING POULTRY SUCCESSFULLY
by Will Graves

"An easy-to-understand beginner's guide to raising chickens, ducks, and geese. A good choice . . ."
Library Journal

Complete how-to for raising meat only, eggs only or a dual purpose flock. Warmly and expertly written.

196 pages, 6×9, illustrations, photos, tables.
Quality paperback, $8.95.

RAISING RABBITS SUCCESSFULLY
by Bob Bennett

"Here is one of the better books on raising rabbits."
Booklist

Written by one of the foremost rabbit authorities, this book is ideal for the beginning rabbit raiser, raising for food, fun, shows and profit.

192 pages, 6×9, illustrations and photos.
Quality paperback, $8.95.

KEEPING BEES
by John Vivian

Noted homesteader John Vivian packs his book with everything the beekeeper needs to know. Plenty of how-to including building your own hives, stands and feeders.

238 pages, 6×9, illustrations and step-by-step photos.
Quality paperback, $10.95.

SUMMER IN A JAR: MAKING PICKLES, JAMS & MORE
by Andrea Chesman

"With recipes this simple and varied, it's hard to find an excuse not to preserve summer in one's cupboard."
Publishers Weekly

Chesman introduces single jar recipes so you can make pickles and relishes a single quart at a time. Plenty of low-sugar jams, marmalades, relishes. Pickles by the crock, too. Outstanding recipes.

160 pages, 8¼×7¼, illustrations.
Quality paperback, $7.95.

GOLDE'S HOMEMADE COOKIES
by Golde Hoffman Soloway
"Cookies are her chosen realm and how sweet a world it is to visit."
Publishers Weekly

Over 100 treasured recipes that defy description. Suffice it to say that no one could walk away from Golde's cookies without asking for another . . . plus the recipe.

144 pages, 8¼×7¼, illustrations.
Quality paperback, $7.95.

THE BROWN BAG COOKBOOK: NUTRITIOUS PORTABLE LUNCHES FOR KIDS AND GROWN-UPS
by Sara Sloan
Here are more than 1,000 brown bag lunch ideas with 150 recipes for simple, quick, nutritious lunches.

192 pages, 8¼×7¼, illustrations.
Quality paperback, $8.95.

HOME TANNING & LEATHERCRAFT SIMPLIFIED
by Kathy Kellogg
"An exceptionally thorough and readable do-it-yourself book."
Library Journal

192 pages, 6×9, step-by-step illustrations, photos, tanning recipes.
Quality paperback, $8.95.

To Order

At your bookstore or order directly from Williamson Publishing. Send check or money order to *Williamson Publishing Co., Church Hill Road, P.O. Box 185, Charlotte, Vermont 05445*. Please add $1.50 for postage and handling. Satisfaction guaranteed or full refund without questions or quibbles.